CONSCI... TO A LASTING LOVE

CONSCIOUS JOURNEY TO A LASTING LOVE

7 PROVEN STEPS TO ATTRACT TRUE LOVE AND BUILD A FULFILLING RELATIONSHIP

By
Xiaoli Mei

This book is dedicated to:

My husband, Jim. You are the love of my life. I traveled across two continents and spent two decades of searching. Finally, our paths crossed.

My two wonderful children Michael and Athena. You are the best gifts life has ever given to me. I am forever grateful.

All women who are still in the dark and seeking the light to find a happy, joyful, and lasting relationship.

DISCLAIMER

This book is not intended as a substitute for the advice of traditional therapists. The reader should regularly consult a therapist in matters relating to his/her mental health and particularly with respect to any symptoms that may require diagnosis or medical attention.

I have tried to recreate events, locales, and conversations from my memories of them. To maintain their anonymity in some instances, I have changed the names of individuals and places; I may have changed some identifying characteristics and details such as physical properties, occupations, and places of residence.

TABLE OF CONTENTS

PREFACE

DOES HAPPILY EVER AFTER EXIST?

RELATIONSHIP SCULPTS OUR SOUL
– TONY ROBBINS

In working with many women over the years, I have observed an interesting fact: no matter what cultural background or educational level, many women have a fantasy about love. Often, that fantasy involves a scenario such as finding a prince charming, falling in love, getting married, having children, and living happily ever after.

I have always pondered the question: Is this love fantasy an inherited instinct or programmed within us by society?

I was born during the Cultural Revolution era in China. All Western influence was strictly prohibited. TV was nonexistent for ordinary families in China at that time. Children had no cartoons to watch, and the result was that, like me, most never became a fan of animated movies or cartons. I don't remember a single Barbie or other doll from my childhood. Luckily, my dad had several Hans Christian Andersen and Grimm's books full of Fairy Tales. I even guess that my own love fantasy stems from reading about princes and princesses, stories that planted seeds in my mind about how love is supposed to be.

But in reality, it didn't happen that way.

I grew up in a culture where boys were trained to be successful and to carry the family name. Girls were similarly trained. But in their case, success meant that they should marry well, take care of their husbands, and raise children. I have a younger brother. My parents always put him first, placing emphasis on his education over mine, and giving him the bulk of their attention. As a young girl, I became highly competitive, focusing on being the best in everything possible, so I could earn more attention and love from my parents. I wanted to prove to my family and society that women can also be successful academically and professionally. After I obtained a Law degree in college, as one of many ambitious women, I decided to come to the US to pursue an advanced education degree, another example of my yearning for more success in life.

Even without any friends or family members here in the US, it didn't take me long to build a life here with an established career in corporate America. Somehow, my personal life did not keep up. With two failed marriages and several botched dating experiences, I felt miserable. Despite the success I achieved in my career, I felt empty, lonely, and confused. I realized that a great career couldn't bring me the total joy and personal happiness I envisioned.

Every breakup, in turn, decreased my self-value and eroded my confidence. With ever-increasing self-doubt, I began to believe that maybe I could not have both a good career and a happy relationship. I questioned my self-worth: Maybe I am not beautiful enough? Maybe I don't deserve to be loved? Maybe it's my destiny? Truly, I started questioning if true love ever existed and if there was such a thing as an intimate relationship.

I started to envy some women who were happily married for years, even though they might not have the highest educational degree or successful career or a Hollywood movie star look, wondering were they just lucky? Or, was I missing something?

At this point in my life, I remember one time, I went to Macy's to do some shopping. A sales lady was helping me with my purchase. She was not the sexy type as I would have defined sexy. She was a bit chubby, with practically every finger decked in flashy jewelry, and a loud talker. But I have to say that her energy was amazing and contagious. She was consistently bubbling, laughing, and making funny jokes. I was so curious and asked her why she was so happy. She said, "Why not? I can't think of a reason not to be happy. I have a wonderful life." I was thinking to myself that she was just a salesperson in Macy's. I knew they didn't get paid well. In what way could she be so happy? I asked her why. "My husband adores me!" she said and pointed to one of her rings. "Last week, we went dancing, and I lost my wedding ring. He just bought me another one without hesitation, I am blessed."

My interaction with the sales lady that day really made me think. Maybe happily ever after really has nothing to do with looks, education, wealth, or a successful career. Likewise, thinking about those gorgeous Hollywood movie stars who have fame, money, looks, and success. Yet, so many of them are not happy, I'm constantly hearing about their never-ending breakups or divorce news.

What is happiness? Does happily ever after really exist? I was determined to find out. I started a journey to search for answers...

I really thought I would find it quickly. But, as it turned out, it was a journey lasting two decades. It started with reading one book and grew quickly to over 100 books, as well as attending numerous workshops and seminars. It was a journey of learning and enlightenment, guided by mentors and coaches, which helped me overcome my own self-doubts and frustrations and made me the person I am today. The answer is like the layers of an onion. You peel back one layer, and you think that you have found the answer. But as you look back at the onion, you realize there is another layer underneath, and another layer to unfold. Life is truly a lifelong adventure in learning!

When I met my soulmate, Jim, many of my friends said I was lucky to meet such a wonderful gentleman. I always tell them there was no luck involved. It was purely through my determination, persistence, and years of self-mastery and discovery that I was able to meet Jim and, together, we created what we have today.

Today, it has become my passion to help women like myself to transform their love life. Over the years, I have met many professional women who are suffering and struggling as I did in my attempt to find love and a happy relationship. It hurts me to see many of them give up after experiencing broken hearts, knowing that for them, love and happiness are within reach.

As for many well-educated emigrated women, our common experience is that we moved from one culture and one language into another. It is easy to feel overwhelmed and confused in such a new and unfamiliar environment. Many times, within our family or our close circle of friends, we do not find the necessary support to really create breakthroughs in relationships because of those old traditions, limiting beliefs, and cultural conflicts. Often, we feel confused, stuck, and trapped between what would be truly good for our happiness and what our cultural traditions have programmed within us. Our old traditions and our new environment conflict. We want to honor the old ways, but perhaps they no longer serve our souls and spirits. But I know it is totally possible to bridge the culture gap, not only in the business world but also in relationship dynamics. It is possible to find a relationship that is not only secure and safe but also full of passion and romance. It is possible to have the love we have always craved since we were little girls. We can break through the cultural imprints on us!

This book will definitely bring hope and light to those women who are still in the dark, cannot see the light, or who are seeking guidance.

This book offers a unique and modern version of "happily ever after" for smart, ambitious, professional women who have spent their life achieving success in their career, yet experience stress and an overwhelmingly empty feeling of missing out on a loving relationship. There are many women who think being independent and successful can bring happiness, but they eventually realize that a successful career does not guarantee a happy relationship. Love and a successful relationship are necessary components to achieving full happiness in life. Being loved and adored, while also returning love to your partner, can fill that void. But achieving success in finding love takes knowledge and understanding.

We were never taught in school or by our parents about the intricacies of love and relationships. We always assumed "happily ever after" came naturally as long as we fell in love and got married. But we never fully understood what falling in love really meant. Understanding human nature and the actions necessary to achieve success in relationships are learnable skills. Happily ever after does exits, but it takes conscious learning and actions.

I am hopeful that by reading about my personal journey and insights, as well as hearing about the journeys of other women I encountered along the way will give you the roadmap for your own personal journey to find happiness in this life.

Although each chapter is relatively independent, I suggest reading each chapter, taking time to digest the concepts & principles, completing the exercise within the chapter, and to take some notes while reflecting on your own experience before moving to the next chapter. Doing so will broaden your understanding of the needs of a relationship from both perspectives, yours and your partner's.

CHAPTER 1

BREAKTHROUGH RELATIONSHIP PATTERNS

"YOUR TASK IS NOT TO SEEK FOR LOVE, BUT MERELY TO SEEK AND FIND ALL THE BARRIERS WITHIN YOURSELF THAT YOU HAVE BUILT AGAINST IT."
– RUMI

"MY LIFE SEEMED TO BE A SERIES OF EVENTS AND ACCIDENTS. YET WHEN I LOOK BACK, I SEE A PATTERN."
—BENOÎT B. MANDELBROT

The Menninger Clinic suggests that there is a 90/10 principle in relationships: 90% of pain, triggers, or reactions within our current relationships are related to experiences from our childhood and past relationships. Only 10% is related directly to our current partners.

Many times, two people love each other. But as the relationship proceeds, each participant unconsciously brings perceptions or wounds from their past experience into their present relationship. Thus, each triggers a reaction in the other without knowing why.

Or, we have rules and expectations in the relationship that stem from our traditional upbringing, and those factors became our rules or expectations in relationships. When our partners do not follow our expectations or rules, we believe they don't love us, or we try so hard to change them, which causes the bottlenecks in the relationship.

I did not see my relationships running a pattern until I broke two marriages and experienced several failed short-term relationships. It seemed I was good at attracting emotionally unavailable men into my life. They were all highly intelligent, business savvy, and successful in what they did. But when it came to intimacy within the relationship, I felt there was a wall between our hearts. Years later, I realized it was because I had a wall around my own heart, and I unconsciously attracted those men into my life. First, I needed to fully understand this part of my life to help me break through my pattern. It was in a moment of consciousness that I realized my parents' relationship dynamics had influenced my own relationship pattern.

My parents were both well-educated at top universities within China. My dad held a high government position and was well respected within his field. My mom was an engineer. But at home, they acted like enemies to each other, consistently in a Cold War. My dad was a typical emotionally unavailable man. As soon as they had a disagreement, he would leave, slamming the door as he left. He would treat us like military soldiers, demanding that we do exactly what he asked us to do at exactly that moment in time. No questions asked. If we did not obey immediately, he would get angry and yell at us. My younger brother and I were always afraid of him as young children.

My mom was a typical traditional Chinese woman. She never talked back, did not like confrontation, was always hiding her true emotions and putting a fake smile on her face in order to act like she was happy. But, on the inside, she was not happy. I could not see it, but I could sense it. In memories, my parents had a few big fights, but most of the time, they just didn't talk to each other. Sometimes the silence lasted for months.

I always felt it was cold and hard to breathe in my family environment. I dreamed and hoped to leave home soon. When I was able to go to college, I left home and stayed in the college dorm as long as I could. After college, I ventured out on my own, vowing to stay away and create my own life out from under their roof.

But whether I liked it or not, either consciously or unconsciously, that childhood experience imprinted on me. When I married the first time, I acted exactly like my mom. How could I not? It was what I learned growing up. It was hard for me to express my uncomfortable feelings or my needs to my first husband. I would avoid any conflicts at all cost without confronting with him. The only difference between my mom and I was I couldn't pretend to be happy, I couldn't smile when I was not happy. So he could see every emotion I experienced and could read from my facial expressions that I was not happy. Can you guess what he did in those instances? He ran away, also avoiding the confrontation. This action made me even more upset. Of course, there were several explosive episodes with big fights between us. When I left China and came to the US to pursue my master's degree, our marriage quickly fell apart.

Divorce is not an emotionally pleasant journey. Like most human beings, I did not enjoy pain. Especially the pain that comes from a divorce. I had to understand where the marriage and where our relationship had failed. I started reading books, studying relationships, and eventually, I believed I learned what went wrong. Yet, even though I was living in a foreign country, my heart still yearning for a family.

When I started dating my second husband-to-be, I thought I would know better after having read so many books and pondering what had caused my first marriage to falter. He came on strong for me in the beginning and was doing all the right things to win my heart. I fell for him quickly and believed I had finally found someone who loved me and would try everything to make me happy. After some time together, I began to notice that he would do anything I asked him to do as long as I did not talk about my emotions. Again, I felt there was a wall between us. There was no connection between our hearts. But by this time, our daughter was on the way. So I stayed in the relationship. After a while, I had the same feeling that I had in my first marriage. I couldn't breathe, and it was a very cold atmosphere at home. I decided to run away from the unhappy marriage. I asked for a divorce.

After being alone for a few years, I started dating again. Interestingly, I kept attracting the same type of men like my dad or my ex-husbands into my dating life. They were intelligent, smart, and successful in what they did, but they were always emotionally unavailable. Every time I would have an emotional outburst, I would end up driving them away. It became a perpetual circle, constantly repeating with each new relationship until I realized I needed to do something different.

I began searching for help. I needed to find someone who would be able to help me break this pattern. I met my first mentor, Peter Hughes. He is a spiritual teacher and a reiki master. He started helping me to see my pattern in relationships and to understand what the root cause was that was interfering with my ability to achieve a happy relationship. It took time for me to discover the unhealthy pattern that was sabotaging my relationships. It also took personal effort to overcome those patterns.

Changing a negative pattern does not happen overnight. But the very first step is to become self-aware of the patterns in your relationships. I also learned that to attract an emotionally available man, I had to learn how to open up my own emotions and how to become vulnerable myself. While I have learned quite a lot over the last several years, I know that I am still learning and mastering even now. Sometimes, when I have a disagreement with Jim, I will still habitually become quiet and begin to suppress my feelings. My wonderful husband will come to me, hold me tight, and ask me, "I love you, baby, tell me what's wrong." Jim is very capable of expressing his feelings. When I am upset or have gone quiet, he will step up for me as a man. He convinces me to expose myself and talk through the emotions I am feeling. Sometimes, the talks can be uncomfortable or painful, but we understand that it is only through communicating our inner feelings can we resolve what is causing the issues in the relationship. Remaining quiet only allows those issues to fester and grow in size. They must be addressed as soon as they come up in the relationship.

Lizzy's Story

In my coaching practice, I have met some clients who had very restricted & critical parents. When they became adults, they were afraid of making mistakes, but at the same time, critical of themselves. In their relationships, they could not stand their partners' imperfections and would end up consistently criticizing their partners' actions. They were acting out as their parents had done with them, based on what they had learned as a child growing up.

Lizzy didn't get much love from her parents while growing up. Her parents were only concerned with her studies and were focused on what kind of top school she should attend. They were highly critical of her as she progressed from high school and into college. She was extremely smart and intelligent academically. She graduated from the top university in China at the top of her class and came to the US to earn her master's degree. Yet, her parents continued to be critical of her choices. Like me, she had failed many times in achieving an intimate relationship. When we started working together, I found out she was very critical of others, and likewise, of herself. As a 42-year-old woman, she would still feel paralyzed in front of her mother. When talking with her mother, she still would feel afraid she would make mistakes. In her intimate relationships, she would constantly criticize her partners and blame them for wrong behaviors. This would cause friction between her and her partner. Most of the time, her partners could not handle her constant criticizing and would withdraw from the relationship. As soon as the man began pulling away, she would begin chasing after him. Even though she was extremely unhappy within the relationship and dissatisfied with the partner she selected, she did not have the courage to leave. She was afraid to start over again in the search for a new soulmate. Therefore, she was tortured between being unhappy and being alone. What she could not see was that her upbringing was carried into her current relationship, and that the relationship could improve drastically if she could redirect her unhappiness at the actions of her partner in a more productive manner. She had that empty void and was wishing her partner could fill it for her. Yet she used her criticizing mechanism as a way to try and get her partner to comply with her wishes.

In working with Liz, I encouraged her to talk a lot about her childhood memories, guiding her to see the way she was conditioned to form her pattern of thinking and behaviors in the relationship with herself and her partners. The biggest breakthrough she achieved was when she finally broke free from that frightened little girl that was inside her from childhood. When she realized that she was no longer that little girl from the past, but an adult who could take responsibility and accountability for her own actions, and not needing the approval of her mother, she became free. From that moment, Liz became an adult, learning to accept herself completely. In return, she became more accepting and understanding of her partner.

Holly's Story

Another type of client I encounter quite often are those who grew up in a family without much love. For these clients, both parents were either too busy just trying to make a living or were dealing with their own troubles. Due to a lack of love and focus from their biological caretakers, the boys grew up to become emotionally unavailable men. They didn't learn how to love others. The girls would grow up to become sensitive and emotionally needy women who crave for love and attention all the time.

Holly always becomes very needy as soon as she is in a relationship with a man. She demanded her partner put her as the top priority in his life. She would constantly check his phone to make sure he was not talking to other women. Any interaction with another woman would send her into a fit of jealousy. If she were not the top priority, she would get upset and lash out at her partner. This would happen weekly. Alex, her partner at the time I began working with her, had two children from his previous marriage. Holly had a hard time accepting that Alex's children were an important part of his life. She would demand that he put her needs as a priority ahead of his own children. She expected him to ALWAYS drop what he was doing and immediately respond to her needs, even if it meant ignoring the basic needs of his children. Alex couldn't understand why she was constantly upset. Even though Alex was attracted to her beauty and intelligence and was very much in love with her, the constant need to satisfy her every outburst for attention began to overshadow the intimacy of the relationship. Gradually he started to withdraw emotionally and began to put distance between Holly and himself. This would make Holly even more upset. Through our work together, Holly realized that the lack of love from her childhood made her always feel insecure in her active relationships. We also uncovered a second roadblock. When she was only six years old, her father left her mother for another woman. From this childhood experience, Holly was always afraid that her men would leave her for another woman.

In Holly's case, we worked on how she could learn to love herself first without looking for love outside. It took Holly nearly a year to really reprogram her mind to accept the fact that she is an amazing person with so much value. Regardless of lacking love from her childhood, she learned how to nurture her self-worth and bring all the love she needs from within.

While it is important to understand how our parent's relationship dynamics impacted us, it is equally important to not blame our parents or resent them. It is highly probable that they learned from their own parents. I am sure our parents believed they were doing their best, pulling from their own experiences and upbringing. By fully understanding our own upbringing and by identifying their impacts on our current relationship patterns and dynamics, we will begin to understand ourselves. Our actions are based on our emotions and what triggers us. We must seek out and find solutions to cure those triggers and break through the patterns. It is only through our efforts to break the pattern that it will not go to the next generation.

It is equally important to understand our past experiences and not to think of ourselves as a victim of the past. It is really our search to understand ourselves better. Interestingly, we tend to look for and attract partners who will trigger the deepest pain within us. Subconsciously, we are looking for an opportunity to heal the wounds from our past. It's almost as if the universe is giving us a second chance to correct and complete the unfinished business of our childhood. When the pattern begins repeating, it is a big signal that we have unfinished business from our childhood. Now it's the time to have a breakthrough and set ourselves free from the past. Finding a good partner will help you to heal.

Lisa's Story

Lisa's ex-husband cheated on her. After her divorce, she didn't want to date for many years. Finally, she met a man, Ken, who loves and adores her. Even though she feels love for him and senses that he loves her completely, she would still get anxious every time when he looked at his phone or began texting someone. The old memories came back of how her ex-husband was texting other women while with her. When Lisa came to me for advice, I encouraged her to share her feelings with her man. She was extremely reluctant because she felt ashamed of admitting that her ex-husband cheated on her. It made her feel that she was not good enough, that's why he went for another woman. Lisa took the courage to tell Ken why she was nervous whenever Ken was on the phone texting. To her surprise, Ken assured her that he would not hesitate to show her who he was texting, giving her full access to everything on his phone. Ken was fully confident in the relationship and had nothing to hide. Through open communication, both Ken and Lisa were able to resolve the insecurity and pain from a past relationship. Now they are happily married. It is no longer an issue for Lisa when Ken is on the phone because he is open to her needs, and she has the confidence to trust him.

In my experiences with my clients, I find that people are not willing to share their past negative experiences or feelings with their new partners because they feel ashamed or afraid their new partner with look down on them. To be intimate in a relationship, it is all about sharing our deepest feelings and vulnerabilities. It takes courage to open up to your partner, but you must know that there are two very good benefits:

- By sharing your past and your own vulnerabilities, you release your old emotions, which will make you will feel lighter and alive. Any emotions that remain suppressed or buried will never die.
- By opening up, you will also see if your new partner has the capacity to handle emotions and your past.

Personally, I always had a fear about my man coming home late. As a child, all I could remember was my dad always came home very late. My mom was the one who would spend time with my brother and me, telling bedtime stories and snuggling us to sleep. When I grew older, my mom told me that my dad was having an affair with another lady in his company. This grew into my own insecurity when my first husband began to come home late. He liked to play Mahjong. It is a very common game in China. On some occasions, he would play the game all night long and would come home in the morning. While I knew he was not having an affair, I could not release the childhood insecurity. I could not sleep and would listen to the cars passing by on the street in the middle of the night in the hope that he would come home soon. I remember standing on the balcony in the dark waiting for him, my mind wondering, "Is this really what marriage is supposed to be like? How come it's so different from what I read in novels and see in movies?" Yet, I also avoided the confrontation of asking him to come home at a reasonable hour.

When I met Jim, that fear was still inside me. Jim tends to be much focused and can sometimes be a workaholic. He likes to work until the job is done. When he starts working on something, he tends to forget everything else. He becomes so focused that time becomes lost to the task. Sometimes in these instances, he would work very late. While he would warn me that he would be home late, he would not be able to tell me how late he would be and what time he would get home. I found on several occasions that this action triggered my old memories. My mind would begin thinking of the worst scenarios as the stories of my past childhood and first marriage started building up in my head. Yet, I was afraid to express my feelings to Jim since it was early in our dating. Even though I told myself to act mature, remain calm, and act like there was nothing wrong, my face could not hide my true emotions. Jim could read it directly from my facial expressions and body language. He knew there was something wrong. So Jim asked me, "Are you okay? Tell me what's wrong." While I initially did not want to bring up my past, I finally found the courage to share my memories and my experiences with Jim. To my surprise, he said, "I am sorry to hear that you had those horrible experiences. Is there anything I can do that will make you feel more secure?" At that moment, I felt I was truly being heard and not being judged for how I felt. I realized that by communicating my feelings with him, and with him being able to communicate back in a loving manner, I could really trust him. This was the beginning of my breaking the emotional roadblock of my past. Today, the "coming home late syndrome" no longer exists for me.

To break the cycle from the past will not only set us free, it will also benefit our next generation through our children and their children. We are the role models for our children. They will tend to act the same way that we act.

Grace's story

Grace's mother always called her "stupid" while she was growing up. Grace believed her mother. "No matter what I do, I'll never measure up." Her mom's verbal abuse caused shame in Grace. To cope, she blocked her own emotional feelings. She would never feel good enough about herself, which greatly impacted her relationships with men. She would try to please men to get their love. Much worse, as a single mom, she was doing the same thing to her own daughter. She said that her intention was to motivate her daughter into doing better. But, in reality, she was tearing down her own daughter's self-worth, as her mother had done to her. Her own daughter did not want to try anything new and was afraid of making mistakes and proving that Grace was right in calling her "stupid." Grace realized how her pattern was already impacting her daughter. In seeing this negative value manifest in her daughter, she was extremely motivated to change the pattern. Through coaching and self-reflection, she was able to overcome this pattern in six short months.

Whatever happened to us in the past, we cannot change it, but we can change what will happen next. Tony Robbins said, "Life is happening for us, not to us." The events of our lives shape us. However, it is the choices we make that define who we are! Never use your past experiences as an excuse not to change or grow. No matter what happened in the past, we are responsible for our own life right now. There is a saying, "You can't stop the wind from blowing, but you can adjust your sail to reach your destiny."

After we understand what the past has done to shape us and the impact it had on our childhood upbringing, then self-parenting becomes critical:

"As a child, I needed a parent's love, nurturing, and emotional maturity to fulfill my emotional dependency needs. As an adult, I still seek to get my emotional dependency needs met, but know I must get my needs met from 'within.' I am a child who has gone from needing a parent's love to needing God's love; from wanting toys to wanting peace and emotional maturity!" – UNKNOWN

Once you release your negative thoughts and emotions, there will be a space for you to create a new experience. In order to create a new experience, you will need to break your old way of doing things. By not breaking those old ways, you will remain stuck in the past and in the negative environment.

As human beings, we look for familiarity and want to be safe. We tend to avoid pain and risk as we seek to do things that make us feel comfortable. We know these past actions did not result in a positive outcome or relationship, and we even know it does not work, but it's the only way we know. If you keep doing the same things over and over, the results will be the same. Now is the time to break the pattern ... to do things DIFFERENTLY!

The best and fastest way to break an old pattern is to identify a mentor or coach who can help you see the things you cannot readily see. They help you to identify any negative thoughts and emotions. Sometimes, it might only need one or two sessions to totally break the chain of your past. Other times, it may take more to identify and break the pattern.

I had a client who grew up in a dysfunctional and broken family. There was always an empty feeling inside her. She spent her entire life looking for love. As a result, she entered into and failed in many relationships. She was chasing the wrong type of men over and over again, seeking to find "love" from them. She looked down on her self-worth and had no guardrails to protect herself from being used. The men she met were not worthy of her, but she could not see it. As a result, these men ended up cheating on her over and over again. She did not know how to protect herself from the hurt caused form her failed dating life. She was continuously living in a hopeless and helpless situation, constantly seeking love. It literally only took us two sessions to help her heal, calming the frightened little girl inside her. For the first time in her life, she felt what it was like to be loved by herself. She became a grown up, strong, and self-content woman. When we finished her breakthrough session, she told me she felt a heavy chain had been broken, and the healing power was inside her. This was a momentous occasion in her life. Finally, she put her broken family behind her, knowing her family doesn't represent who she is, and she would not live in the shadow of her broken family and continue to feel ashamed.

With conscious learning and the right guidance, creating the love you want does not have to be a hard journey.

> *When I break pattern,*
> *I break ground.*
> *I rebuild when I break down*
> *I wake up more awake*
> *Than I've ever been before*
> "Pluto" by Sleeping At Last

CHAPTER 1 SUMMARY

- All things have patterns. If our relationship didn't work well, mostly, there were some patterns that prevented us from being successful
- The first step to break through patterns is to be aware of them
- 90% of our relationship pain, triggers, or reactions are related to our experience from our childhood and past relationships. Only 10% is related directly to our current partners

- To understand how our parent's relationship dynamics impacted us is not to blame our parents or resent them
- To understand our upbringing and how it developed into our current relationship patterns and dynamics will help us to understand ourselves, our emotions, and what triggers us

CHAPTER 1 EXERCISE: SELF REFLECTION

Write down all your past relationships that worked and those that didn't. This will help you to identify your patterns:

- What kind of people or relationships do you keep attracting, and ask why.
- What were your emotional needs that were not being met when you were a child?
- What negative emotions do you remember having as a child?
- What are some key decisions you made about yourself or about life as a child?
- Do you know your emotional triggers?
- What things are you ashamed to talk about and why?

Once you realize the patterns, it will be easy to break through it. If it's hard to do on your own, you can always ask for professional help.

CHAPTER 2

POWER OF BELIEFS

WE ARE WHAT WE THINK – JAMES ALLEN

In China, even today, high school students in
Grade 12 have to take a national exam to qualify
for college. It was a very intense process both for
parents and students. In the US, colleges will look
at your GPAs and SAT scores. But in China, we do
not have a GPA system. Every year in June, all
Grade 12 students will take this national exam
comprised of all the subjects taught in school. The
education department announces what score is
required to qualify for entering college. If your
score is below the cutoff line, you will not be able

to attend a 4-year college. It seems for Chinese children, their future destiny really depends on this exam. When I first took the exam, my score came below the college cutoff line. I was very disappointed in myself. But I really wanted to go to college, so I asked my parents if I could retake the exam the following year, which meant I had to stay in high school for one more year to study. My dad said, "No! We do not have that kind of money to spend. Plus, you are a girl. Eventually, you will get married and leave the house. Why don't you find a job to reduce some family burden?" I cried for days. My mom wanted to support me, so she had a big fight with my dad. Finally, he agreed. That whole year, it was painful to stay at home and see my dad's angry face every day. He kept telling me, "You might find it hard to find a good husband if you spend more time chasing this advanced degree dream."

The next year, I passed the exam and was accepted into a law degree program by a university. I studied extra hard to prove to my parents that I was capable of succeeding. Four years later, I graduated as the No. 1 top student in law school. Our school Dean came to talk to me and encouraged me to pursue a master's degree. At that point, my dad's belief and statements from the previous year really played out in my head. I was afraid if I pursued a master's degree, it would be hard to find a husband, get married, and have a family. So I said, "NO."

Thinking back, it's such a naïve belief. But I am not alone. Talking to many other women over the years, I found that some of them still have that kind of belief; "If I became too successful, it would intimidate my partner and ruin the relationship."

Another belief I had was related to finding love. After years of kissing many frogs and not being able to turn them into a prince, I started to doubt myself. I began to ask myself, "Was something wrong with me? Was I not lovable? Maybe, I am not pretty enough?" When I was older, my mom even added to my self-doubt, saying all the good quality men around my age were either taken or would be more interested in younger, prettier women. That made me add another false belief; that I was too old to find a good quality man. She always reminded me that, "it's hard to find a man when you already have two children. Who will take a woman who has children from another man?"

It didn't feel very good to hear it. Especially from my own mother. It had a sense of disempowering control over me. I felt like I was emotionally done. I was damaged. I could never find happiness.

One of the biggest turning points in my life was when my mentor, Peter, introduced me to the concept of the Law of Attraction. In the New Thought philosophy, the Law of Attraction is the belief that positive or negative thoughts bring positive or negative experiences into a person's life. The belief is based on the idea that people and their thoughts are both made from pure energy, and that through the process of energy attracting like energy, a person can improve their own health, wealth, and personal relationships.

At the same time, I also discovered "Abraham Hicks Teaching" by Jerry and Ester Hicks. (https://www.abraham-hicks.com/about/) It was an eye-opening discovery for me to understand Universal Laws and how our beliefs in either positive or negative energy shape our reality. Whatever we believe to be true, we will experience. Our ego mind will supply us with any evidence that we need to support our beliefs.

I realized my own negative beliefs created my own experience. If I let those beliefs continue to run my life, my life would still remain the same old experience. I was determined to follow Peter's coaching to change my thinking patterns and beliefs. Only after I liberated myself from those limiting beliefs, did my life started to change and lead me to meet the love of my life. He is everything I was looking for and contrary to my belief about men only wanting much younger women. When I took Jim to visit my mom, she was surprised and wondered how I found this handsome looking guy who was my age.

My friends said I was lucky to get the right guy. But I have to tell you that I had been single for more than 10 years before I met him. In those years, I struggled with exactly the same things you might be going through now... all the frustrations, fears, and doubts. I struggled with them too. But once I overcame my own limiting beliefs, I created new beliefs about love, and I quickly attracted new experiences into my love life. Because it is such a powerful concept, I started teaching my clients how to use the Law of Attraction and the power of beliefs to create the loving relationship we yearned for in our lives.

Identify Your Limiting Beliefs

What is a belief? An acceptance that a statement we make is true. Most of us formed our beliefs based on our own life experience or influence from people around us. From our experience, we tend to think that the outcomes are the truth. Psychologists estimate that over 90% of our beliefs are unconscious, and that most of our unconscious beliefs were created as a result of thoughts that we were programmed to believe. Whatever we believe, it controls our behaviors. Behaviors create our reality. So it's hard to see past our own limiting beliefs without some guidance. When women come for coaching, they know something is not working. But a majority of them do not know that it is their pattern of thinking that is not serving them well, and that is preventing them from achieving the results they wanted. My role is to help them identify their limiting beliefs. In pursuing their own intimate relationship, many women have common beliefs such as, "I am not slim enough," "I am too old," "I am not pretty or I am not good enough," "Maybe I don't deserve love." Each of these statements is a false limiting belief. They should NOT hold power over the relationship you deserve.

Release Limiting Beliefs

Since we understand negative beliefs only attract negative experience, and once we identify our limiting beliefs, the next natural step is to learn how to release them. In coaching, I am often asked by my clients how exactly to release the negative beliefs. I always wished there was a magic wand to wipe out all the negative beliefs, creating room for new positive beliefs to automatically drop in. But that's not the way our minds work. Most of our unconscious beliefs were created as a result of thoughts that we were programmed to believe. The only way to replace the negative limiting believes is by re-programming ourselves.

It takes discipline and repetition to reprogram our beliefs. In the beginning, you might use an affirmation technique. For example, you may write, "I am lovable. I am beautiful. I deserve to be loved." But you may find that just writing those words will not work. In your subconscious mind, you may still feel it is not true. Having a coach is key to getting you started and guiding you on the path to believing. It is up to you to practice daily and to totally transform your beliefs, but it is also necessary to find support in overcoming the subconscious mind.

I discovered a self-mastery book written by Joseph Hu Dalconzo. He explained why affirmations alone will not work. He described it by stating, "Doing affirmations alone is like putting on a clean shirt before taking a shower! You will not create permanent positive changes in your life if your mind is still cluttered with contradictory past bad experience." He created these 7 steps to dis-create our negatively programmed beliefs.

---

7 Steps to Help You Dis-Create Your Negatively Programmed Beliefs

---

1. List areas in your life where you have experienced uncomfortable sensations, pain, or loss
2. Identify the top ten areas of pain in your life, then pinpoint the top three
3. Using the list of your top three areas of pain, begin to surface your unconscious negative beliefs. Note, when deeper issues surface, try to follow them to the root cause or source of your original pain. Record your negative beliefs in a journal
4. Twice a week, for three to six weeks after a negative belief surfaces, read it out loud to keep it consciously surfaced so that you can hear when you are negatively sub-vocalizing

5. Train your mind to HEAR AND FEEL when it begins to sub-vocalize negative belief patterns.

6. Dis-create your negative beliefs by immediately saying the affirmation "I now dis-create. my belief that....."

7. Lastly, affirm what it is you do want to create in your life!

Replace a New Belief

In the universe, no two objects can occupy the same space at the same time. Therefore, to make room for a new belief, we must release an old one. A key component of the Law of Attraction is that to effectively change one's negative thinking patterns, we must feel that the desired changes have already occurred through visualization and meditation. The challenge is sometimes hard for people to form a new positive belief if they all had was a bad experience in the past.

For example, Amy has never married, but has had a few long-term relationships. In those relationships, she would eventually discover that they were either already married or she caught them cheating on her. So, in her belief system, men are all cheaters or liars. She had a hard time believing there are loyal men out there for her to find. In her situation, she needed some positive experiences or role models to help her believe there are good men out there for her. I asked her if someone she knows has a good relationship and been married for a long time. She said one of her best friends has been happily married for many years. I asked her if she knew her friend's husband and what she thinks about this husband. "Is he a good man and loyal?" I asked. "Yes! Without question!" she agreed. Here was a loyal man that was not like all the other cheaters or liars. Could she imagine many other good men out there, just like her friend's husband? Logically, she asked the next question, "Why do I only attract those unfaithful men?" Through guided questions and answers, it became clear to her that it was not a problem with all men. It was with her point of focus and attraction. It was the Law of Attraction. She believed all men were liars and cheaters, so she attracted those same liars and cheaters.

Visualization of the relationship you desire is another way to establish a new belief. Focus on where you want to go! One of the exercises I do with my clients in the beginning is to design a blueprint for their ideal love life. What they want from a relationship, why they want one, and what life would be like when they meet "The One." They must use their entire imagination as they describe what their life will look like one year from now. To detail what it will look like five years from now. How they will feel if they already have this vision of a partner in their life. I ask them to meditate and visualize that blueprint daily.

When they feel frustrated with dating, I always bring them back to their WHY. By focusing on the WHY, it enables them to keep going.

If you are on the journey to look for true love but feel frustrated and disappointed, take some time to think through what limiting beliefs are holding you back. According to the Law of Polarity, everything is dual. So things that appear to be opposites are actually two inseparable parts of the same thing. If we desire for a loving relationship, the outcome is already existing. It is just waiting for us to claim it. The only thing preventing us from seeing and claiming it is our own resistance. Internal resistance... resistance from ourselves, our mind, and our thinking patterns...including some patterns to which we are not even aware. This is a good reason why having a professional coach to guide you is so important for changing your circumstances and bringing you closer to your goal of finding true love. Like my mentor told me, "A coach's work is to keep people from resisting." In my professional experience, I can tell you with certainty that we can change almost everything we believe about our lives in order to improve our lives.

CHAPTER 2 SUMMARY

- Our beliefs are created from our own experience
- Most of us formed our beliefs based on our own life experience or influence from people around us, then we think they are the truth
- Psychologists estimate that over 90% of our beliefs are unconscious, and that most of our unconscious beliefs were created as a result of thoughts that we were programmed to believe
- In the universe, no two objects can occupy the same space at the same time. Therefore, to make room for a new belief, we must release an old belief.

CHAPTER 2 EXERCISE: IDENTIFY YOUR LIMITING BELIEFS

Over the years, I collected the following limiting beliefs from my clients. Take a look, you might identify some of yours from the list:

- I am unlucky in love
- I am unlovable
- My one and only true love left me
- It's too late
- I live in the wrong place
- I am unattractive
- It's not okay to talk about problems
- Feelings should not be expressed openly
- Keep feelings to yourself
- Be strong, right and perfect
- Don't be selfish
- It's not okay to play or be playful
- Don't rock the boat
- Always be doing something meaningful/productive
- Important things are always serious and dramatic
- It's not okay to cry - crying is weak
- I am not so important
- My dreams are ridiculous
- I can't do that
- Don't even think about doing that
- Good things never happen to me or for me....

- I'll never have what I want
- Love is hard
- You have to work hard to get anything you want
- If you open your heart to anyone, you'll get hurt
- Men are no good
- The only way to get attention is to have a serious problem...
- I'll never have what I want, it's just not in the cards or the stars for me
- My mother never had anything good, and so I won't either
- He'll never love me
- He'll cheat on me, they all do
- This will end badly like they all do
- Of course he won't commit to me
- I feel hopeless all the time
- I'm too busy and don't have time to date
- I'm too old/overweight/damaged/in debt
- There are no conscious men out there
- I have limiting beliefs I can't shift
- My career is more important than having a relationship

WRITE DOWN some of your own limiting beliefs that were triggered by the list. Once you identify your limiting belief, you can use the 7 steps in this chapter to help you dis-create your negatively programmed beliefs

CHAPTER 3

BECAME A FEMININE GODDESS

GODDESS: NOUN, A FEMALE GOD; A WOMAN WHOSE GREAT CHARM OR BEAUTY AROUSES ADORATION – MERRIAM-WEBSTER

When I met Diana for the first time, I wasn't sure she came for coaching or just came to make another business deal. She was well dressed, sharp, and edging into her mid-40s. She ran a multi-million-dollar business. Indeed, she was clearly a good catch for any man. Ivy-League educated, super intelligent, plus a sophisticated look! Her challenge was that all the guys she dated were so attracted to her in the beginning but would either not commit to the relationship or would eventually run away from her. It became a big puzzle for her. She could get men easily but could not keep them. I quickly realized what caused her to be in this constant predicament: Her CEO energy. She was unconsciously leading with her masculine energy and dominating the relationship. This masculine energy pushed the men away.

In today's modern society, women are often self-sufficient and independent. They are managers, leaders, CEOs, business owners, entrepreneurs, and directors. In order to lead, we must exert a lot of "masculine energy" to achieve the results we want... in business, in life, and in raising children. We must organize, strategize, and tell others what we need them to do. We make lists and push projects forward. We stay on top of things and "check in" when things aren't going according to schedule. Sometimes it's a must in the workplace. But often, masculine energy totally goes against you in an intimate relationship.

As a human being, we all share energy that is both masculine and feminine. Think of it as Yin and Yang, both complementary and necessary.

Masculine energy is about strength, logic, single focus, result-oriented, steadiness, and a desire to protect. Your masculine side is expressed when you're working toward a goal, making progress, getting things done, and pushing forward. This is important within your professional work and world.

Feminine energy is about being receptive, receiving, soft, allowing, flow, flexibility, emotion, and a desire to nurture. Your feminine side is expressed when you move with the flow of life, embrace your creative energy, dance, play, and attune to your internal process. The feminine is pure presence. It makes us softer, gentler, kinder, nurturing, more compassionate, and naturally loving. This is important in your relationship world.

As women, we naturally have feminine energy. We are created to bond. We are designed for relationships. We are designed to create life. And yes, our soft, gentle features are meant to attract males.

However, in this modern hectic world, when we become overloaded with masculine energy, we spend most of our time working and very little time resting, taking vacations, and spontaneously connecting with others. We have been operating using the masculine energy for so long, we have forgotten how to tap into the feminine energy within. Working in the corporate world for over sixteen years, I see professional women thrive and achieve in business. But they have a hard time deeply connecting with another human being through their hearts and emotions. We tend to stay in our head instead of in our heart.

I conducted a survey to ask a group of women what challenges they experienced most in their love life and relationships. One of the most common things mentioned was that they did not know how to connect with their emotions and express these emotions in an effective way in a relationship. They would have no outlet for these emotions and would accumulate a lot of resentment toward their current or past relationships based on these pent-up feelings.

It's not always obvious to the woman, who has a hard time disengaging from the image she has of herself professionally. There is saying; "CEO mode is dynamic, but not magnetic." That is an exact description of Diana and many other female high achievers. In the love department, we do not need the CEO mode of masculine energy. We need to be who we are as women—feeling, experiencing, and receiving.

Dr. John Gray, in his book *Men from Mars and Women from Venus*, articulated how masculine and feminine energy play out in the intimate relationship. Men's commitment to a relationship has nothing to do with looks, personality, and level of success. It really comes down to what energy women use to approach men and bring to the relationship. Men will admire and respect your independence but would prefer to date feminine women. You don't have to be a CEO, but you might unconsciously carry your masculine energy in dating or a relationship. Men will admire you and respect you for that, but it's not something they look in the intimate setting.

Vivian's Story

Vivian came to me in tears. She found out her husband had cheated on her after only three years of marriage. Vivian is a very successful real estate broker, owning many properties, and is self-sufficient. She is beautiful, charming, and is very business savvy. She talks no nonsense. She doesn't waste time gossiping with other women. Her male-coworkers thinks she is successful but also aggressive. She gets things done with efficiency. She is proud of her professional self and her business accomplishments. But she could not understand why her husband would cheat on her. "I have looks, money, success, what else does he want?" She felt hurt by his betrayal. Yet, Vivian is very demanding. She carried that energy into her marriage. Her husband didn't feel needed and appreciated because she did everything for herself. At one point in the relationship, her husband even commented, "You are so independent, you don't need me, and you don't need men." After learning about masculine and feminine energies and how to apply them effectively, Vivian learned how to consciously balance her masculine energy and feminine energy. She now understands the root cause for this infidelity in her past marriage. Even though the marriage did not work out, she started the process of healing and now uses that feminine energy to appeal to the desires of the male to satisfy her needs.

Other women might not be exactly like Vivian, running their own successful business and satisfying the demands as a CEO. But they may still be carrying the same masculine energy into their own relationship. Men will not fall in love with you if you try to do things for him or always be available for him. Anything you do to try to impress or take care of a man will usually end up having the opposite effect. You will end pushing him away. A common mistake woman make is that they use the same approach that they expect their man to take in the relationship. You should not approach the relationship from a man's perspective. You must use feminine energy, and approach it from that perspective.

Sharon's Story

Sharon is so nice and pleasing. She is so eager to help men and do things for them. She quickly moved herself into her boyfriend's apartment within only a few months into dating him. She was eager to start cooking, doing laundry, and organizing everything for their dates and going out. She was always available whenever he needed her, saying "yes" to the things she really did not want to do. She basically put her life on hold to be available for him. She wanted a commitment and a family so badly. Yet, three years into the relationship, she was frustrated. Her boyfriend still hadn't mentioned a single word about commitment. By doing these things for her boyfriend, Sharon was trying to get something: commitment. But she was not receiving it. She was carrying a lot of resentment for her boyfriend because there was no reciprocation for her actions.

Doing all of these things will not make a man fall in love with you. He may stay in a relationship with you for years because it's convenient for him, but he won't make the final commitment to marry you. He will become lazy because his masculine energy is inactive and is not needed in this type of relationship. He will stop being romantic. You, on the other hand, will become angry, frustrated, and will feel hopeless and not feel loved.

Sharon realized she did not set healthy boundaries and was overcompensating by being controlling and over-pleasing in an attempt to receive love in return. Without boundaries, the relationship cannot flow. It cannot ply the masculine and feminine energies for a positive outcome. Once Sharon identified this as an issue, and she was given the means to set positive boundaries, she was able to turn the relationship into a positive, caring, and healthy one. She is more confident and centered than ever before. She is focused on her own happiness, as well as his, and is doing the things she loves to do. Her boyfriend adores her.

Another type of common situation I see is when women act like they don't need a man. Being single for so long, they will often doubt if they actually need a man or a relationship in their life at all. It seems as if a bad relationship will only bring drama and frustration into their life. Some women are afraid of losing control, fearful that in relinquishing control to a man, it will make them weak. Letting a man lead does not mean you are incapable or unable to be independent. A good partner will give you the space to be who you are, without sacrificing your freedom or independence. Women who were hurt before in a relationship tend to become overprotective of their emotions and needs. Not wanting to be betrayed or hurt again, they do not want to give power and control to the man. When they say, "I don't need a man in my life," it tends to come from a place of fear from previous failed relationships.

Joan's Story

Joan told me she doesn't really need men, but it was nice to have some companionship and have someone to travel with and have fun together. In dating, she was very guarded. She didn't want men to pay for the dates. She preferred to "go Dutch." She said, "I don't want to owe them, so they don't get on my nerves if I decide to break up with them." She complained men were weak and needy. But actually, she attracts men who are always taking advantage of her. These men are "beta" men who are super-sensitive and weak. After a while, Joan would tire of their constant complaining. She would think they were not a man at all. In general, women are easily turned off by passive and submissive men. Occasionally, she would meet a few nice gentlemen, but they would eventually lose interest and fade away after a short time together. She came to ask why this happened to her. "They sensed your 'I don't need men' energy," I told her. "Men want to be your hero. They want your respect and admiration. They didn't receive that from you, and so they went searching elsewhere," I explained.

In working with Joan, we dived deeper to identify her own needs from a relationship, and why she needed a relationship at all. We covered important aspects of the different emotional needs between women and men. Most importantly, how to psychologically understand men in dating and in relationships. Gradually, Joan learned to let her guard down and share her feelings and vulnerabilities. She accepted that she liked needing a man in her life. When we last spoke, she was engaged to a wonderful man and planning her big wedding.

The Dance between Masculine and Feminine

As a human being, we possess both masculine and feminine energy. I am not asking you to totally give up on masculine. All you need to do is consciously balance between your masculine energy and feminine energy in a relationship.

Masculine and feminine polarity cause attraction & passion in a relationship. A man is attracted to your feminine energy. After wearing his armor on the outside competitive world, he wants to come home and enjoy your feminine side, feel needed, appreciated, relaxed, loved, not being blamed, managed, or criticized.

When you embody your feminine side around a man, he will be smitten by you. He will want to shower you with adoration and generosity. When you cling to your masculine energy, a man will find a way to withdraw or disappear.

During my coaching with strong, smart, professional women, here is what I heard a lot from single women: "Why do some men try so hard to chase you at the beginning of dating or relationship. Then, after six months together, they stop trying to please you and begin to take things for granted?"

From married but unhappy women: "Why does my husband not listen? When I talk to him, he will zone out?" "Why does he leave the room when I begin to complain about something?" or "Why has he become so lazy and doesn't help with the house chores? I am the one doing everything around the house! What made him change?"

There are many reasons for the cause of these situations. But I noticed one thing in common: the masculine energy and feminine energy polarity was lost along the way. Opposites can create tension and attraction.

As Dr. John Gray summarized in his book, *Men from Mars and Women from Venus*: "When partners are living in their core energy, they attract naturally. However, when under pressure, they lose their way and take on opposite attributes. When polarity is gone, masculine partners are seen as weak, indecisive, emotional, and ineffective. Feminine partners slip into behaviors that are hardened, inflexible, emotionless, and uncaring."

When strong, smart, and successful professional women bring their masculine energy into relationships, they still act like managers, VPs demanding a result, correcting, managing, achieving. Naturally, men become weak in that type of relationship. Over time, men will give up pleasing, adoring, and making women happy.

Of course, it's not only the women who need to balance this energy polarity in relationships. Men must also learn to bring out their partner's feminine energy by learning how to effectively listen to their woman, how to emotionally support them, and how to calm them down when women get stressed out.

As male and female dynamics, just remember men are naturally providers and protectors, who want to be appreciated, respected, and admired in the relationship, not to be managed. Women are naturally receivers, who want to be heard, loved, cherished, and nurtured.

Being Irresistible To the Relationship

There are two types of attraction: Animal attraction and human spirit attraction.

Animal attraction is more of a physical attraction. Men and women are attracted to each other by the look, body shape, and chemistry.

Human Spirit attraction means men and women are compatible and attractive mentally, emotionally, and spiritually.

We all start from the physical attraction level at the beginning. Each person has his or her own preference and tends to be drawn to certain type of looks and body shapes. It is possible to have more chemistry with some people more than others. There is nothing wrong with that. But we can't stop at the physical level and think that physical attraction will make the relationship last. If that were so, we would not see the drama played out between actors and actresses like we do in the daily news. The secret to being irresistible does not rest on your looks, your age, or your body shape alone.

The human spirit attraction is the second key to make men devoted to you and to the relationship.

For women to be irresistible, we need to switch from our DOING energy and convert it into BEING energy. Doing energy is a very masculine energy. Of course, we need it to get things done in our professional life. We must first be who we really are, then do what we really need to do to have what we want.

What BEING energy looks like:

- Being confident: when we feel confident about ourselves, the strength and the weakness, when we accept ourselves, our imperfection, when we are comfortable at our own skin, we are radiating, we are beaming, and we are in our best feminine state. I meet some women, they are beautiful and smart, but they are constantly feeling not good enough about themselves! Some are too self-critical.

- Being authentic: if you look at the definition of authentic: not false or copies, genuine, real. It says it all. You are the only YOU, no one else will be identical to you. So be true to yourself. Speak what's on your mind. No manipulation, no game playing.

- Being passionate: you probably have no idea how beautiful you are when you are passionate about what you do, about life experience. When you are talking about something you are passionate about, your eyes will sparkle...it's a huge turn on for men!

- Being receptive: Being receptive is the way to a man's heart. Men need you to be receptive, so they are compelled to protect you, provide for you, and care about you. If you understand men and women dynamics, being receptive is the motive for men to please you and make you happy. Let him contribute to you and help you because men take credit for your happiness. They feel successful with you. The only thing they need from you is your appreciation. So let men contribute to you, please and provide for you.

Also being receptive to the man, to his energy. Are you receptive to his values, his needs, and his boundaries?

Tap into Your Feminine Energy

The feminine energy isn't something you have to "do." It is not a process. It is a state of being. This is the most difficult part for high achieving professional women to comprehend because we are so used to this "doing" energy. So our logical mind does not know how to achieve this "being "state.

There are many ways to tap into your feminine energy. Here I share three ways I use most for myself and for my clients;

★ *Through Your Feelings*

Feelings are the intuitive message from our heart. When we resist, repress, or deny our feelings, we disconnect ourselves from our own heart. Feminine energy is about feelings. As women, we need to know how to express our feelings, especially those uncomfortable feelings, without blaming and complaining to our partners. The #1 problem in a relationship is a lack of effective communication. Women don't express their uncomfortable feelings, they repress them, build up resentment, and explode with the upsets in a blaming tone. When we use a blaming tone to talk to our partner, it will push them away because they feel discouraged that they couldn't make us happy. They feel they were not appreciated.

It really took me some time to learn how to express my uncomfortable feelings with my partner. As you know, growing up in a family where feelings were not fully expressed, it was hard to overcome this fear. I had to start from the beginning, like a baby learning to first talk, for me to properly express my feelings to men. It felt scary at the beginning. It is like speaking another language. But through practice and repetition, it became easier and easier. Today, it is very easy for me to express my feelings with my husband. Mastering a new skill is through practice and repetition.

★ *Showing Your Vulnerability*

Sometimes in dating and in a relationship, we are scared to show our vulnerability and afraid that our partner might judge us or won't love us anymore when he sees our weaknesses. That is far from the truth.

Showing your vulnerability is saying, "I am human, I have flaws, and I'm okay with that." Showing your vulnerability may actually bring men closer to you. If you try to be too clean and perfect, men will feel alienated by you and won't want to open up for fear of looking weak in front of you.

Lin had a very messy divorce. It greatly impacted her self-esteem. When she started dating again, she was very guarded but pretended to be happy with lots of smiles. She'd been dating with this guy John for about three months. Things stayed at a very superficial level. She never really talked about herself. One day, when they were on a date, she suddenly had a medical emergency. Her date took her to the nearby hospital. The doctor wanted to do surgery immediately. Her family was far away. Lin was so scared, she grabbed John's hand and kept saying, "I am scared." John stayed with her the whole time. Once the surgery was complete, he would keep coming back to visit her until she was out of the hospital. Since that incident, seeing that being vulnerable did not scare John away, Lin started to open up, her life, her emotions, and her fears to John. Surprisingly to Lin, he started opening up to her as well. Their relationship really moved to the next level with this event. More intimate and profound. Sometimes, the things that happen in life will highlight the true nature of men to want to take care of and protect their partner.

What's truly attractive is a woman who is aware of her character flaws and challenges yet knows how incredible she is anyway. She doesn't care about her little vulnerabilities because she secretly knows how awesome she is overall. Showing your vulnerability takes self-confidence because it doesn't define who you are.

"The Gifts of Imperfection" by Brene Brown is a great book about vulnerability, courage, worthiness, and shame. It explains how to live a wholehearted life and embrace who you are. Brene Brown is a "vulnerability" expert. She has studied shame, vulnerability, and courage for decades. I recommended all my clients to read her books. https://brenebrown.com/

★ *Surrender*

There was a time when I was very frustrated and disappointed that things didn't happen the way I wanted. I complained to my coach. He kept telling me to surrender to the universe. I couldn't understand how to surrender. If you have been operating mostly from your masculine energy, you may have a difficult time surrendering because your head will try to keep control. Surrendering is letting go of the control the mind has on you. It can be scary and intimidating.

Surrender is not a process but an allowing. Surrendering is moving from the head to the heart. Allowing the universe to unfold things organically for us instead of pushing it. It sounds counter-intuitive, but it's a way for our dreams to come true. Tony Robbins once said if you have done massive actions, you have to give grace time. Simply replace the expectation with appreciation.

Most people don't want to surrender because taking away control freaks them out! Surrendering isn't something you need to DO but a place to come FROM. A place that you are. The more you connect to your heart, the more you are in surrender mode.

When you are challenged or feel yourself stuck in your masculine, breathe from the place of surrender. Feel your body fill with light and space. Find the space within you that is free from your judgment of your thoughts and let go. Let go of the need to figure it out, let go of your tight grip on things. Let go of the fight for control. Just breathe and be willing to not know how to surrender! Just be in your willingness for something different!

Surrender is coming from a place of abundance. To believe there is enough for everyone. Things will always find a way to work out. You do not even need to know how it does it. A willingness to let it go is all you need.

★ *Recharge Your Feminine Energy*

Energy is flow. It gets easily depleted. So it needs to be consciously recharged, otherwise, we will experience burnout.

There are many ways to recharge your feminine energy:

- **Reflection**

Many of us are so busy that we rarely take the time to listen to what's going on inside of us. We lose touch with our deeper selves. We need to set the time aside to connect internally to who we are. Mediation, yoga, hiking in nature, or even talking to a coach to explore your inner thoughts and feelings.

- **Nature**

The feminine is life force energy. Places like the forest, jungle, parks, and the ocean are abundant with natural feminine energy. Go there when you're feeling out of sync and in need of revitalization. I always encourage my single clients to go on weekend hiking meetup groups. Not only you can ground yourself, it's a great way to meet new people.

- **Creativity**

The feminine is the creative force. Creation can occur in many ways — artistic expression, writing, dancing, painting, designing. Envision what you want to create. Anything that expresses your flow is considered feminine.

- **Receptivity**

Learning when to initiate and when to allow, rather than habitually launching into action or fix-it mode. You don't have to do it all. By receiving love/energy/attention, your deep well of feminine energy is filled up. Receptivity could be very hard for some women.

- **Dress up**

Dressing up makes me feel feminine. Pick out pretty clothes, get a favorite lipstick color, wear your favorite jewelry, or buy a nice pair of fashionable shoes. Dress up for concerts, romantic dinners, and all the special occasions. One of the favorite things my husband and I enjoy doing is dressing up to attend the symphony or going to fancy dinners.

- **Time with your girlfriends**

When was your last time to spend intentional time with other like-minded women? It's a great way to recharge your feminine energy. When you are exclusively with those of your gender, it's easier to drop the masks and be yourself, as you are, talk without trying to impress.

- **Indulge Your Senses**

One way to connect to our bodies more and get out of logical thinking is to practice incorporating more sensuality into our lives. This means intentionally using the senses to experience life with pleasure.

One way I practice sensuality is by soaking in a warm bath with essential oils. Setting the visual with candles or petals, feeling the warm water against my skin, smelling the aroma of lavender or eucalyptus, hearing the water splash against the tub, tasting a treat like dark chocolate or red wine.

Any activity can become sensual if you intentionally experience it with all five senses.

To re-connect with your feminine energy, indulge your taste buds by eating chocolate, drinking red wine, and indulging your palate with decadent foods that you love. Indulge your sense of touch by going shopping and feeling all of the soft fabrics. You can also go to a public food market and take in all the different sights and smells of the delicious foods surrounding you. Get out of your head and into your body by intentionally living in your senses.

Just remember, when you are deep in your feminine energy, it is this mode when you will feel the beauty of your body; you have fallen in love with yourself; you feel confident about yourself; you are comfortable receiving and letting go of control; you are speaking your truth. You are playful, and you show your vulnerability.

When you are happy, feel confident, and receptive, those are the irresistible qualities to men. So now that you know the secret to attracting men is not about your looks, your body shape, or your success. Now it explains why those Hollywood movie stars who have fame, beauty, money but constantly have heartbreaks.

CHAPTER 3 SUMMARY

- Feminine energy is about receptive, receiving, soft, allowing, flow, flexibility, emotion, and a desire to nurture.
- Your feminine side gets expressed when you move with the flow of life, embrace your creative energy, dance, play, and attune to your internal process.
- When we are overloaded with masculine energy, we can't truly connect with people emotionally.
- Masculine and feminine polarity cause attraction & passion in a relationship.
- Men are naturally providers and protectors, who want to be appreciated, respected, and admired in a relationship, not to be managed. Women are naturally receivers, who want to be heard, loved, cherished, and nurtured.
- The feminine energy isn't something you have to "do." It is not a process but a state of being.

CHAPTER 3 EXERCISE: EXPRESS FEELINGS

Next time you are upset with anyone, instead of suppressing your feelings, speak up by starting with, "I feel..." Then articulate how you feel. No blaming or accusing others; just sincerely state your own feelings. You will be surprised at what happens next. When you are being true to yourself, you can immediately feel a relief and a sense of inner power right there.

CHAPTER 4

BEGIN THE JOURNEY TO YOURSELF

"EMBARK ON THE JOURNEY OF LOVE, IT TAKES YOU FROM YOURSELF TO YOURSELF"
– RUMI

Once, I read an interesting article on the internet talking about a scar experiment: A scientific researcher assembled ten unsuspecting volunteers for a psychological study. The participants were separated into ten different cubicles without mirrors. The purpose of the study was to observe how people would respond to a stranger with a marred physical appearance, such as a facial scar. Using Hollywood makeup tricks, the scientists put bloody and gruesome scars on each volunteer's left cheek, and displayed the new "scar" to each participant using a small handheld mirror. After glancing at their marred image, the mirror was taken away. The researcher's final step was to inform each volunteer that some finishing powder needed to be placed on his/her scar to prevent it from smearing. In reality, the researcher used a tissue to wipe off the scar. But the volunteers still believed they had the awful scars on their faces.

Each individual was sent out into the waiting rooms of different medical offices with instructions to take note of how strangers responded to their appearance. After the appointed time, the ten volunteers returned to the scientific researcher and all shared the same report. In their encounters, they noticed that strangers were ruder to them, less kind, and stared at their scar. In fact, there were no scars on any of the volunteers. Regardless of the removal of the false scars, their unhealthy perspective of themselves affected how they thought others saw them.

https://youthays.wordpress.com/a-z-illustration/the-scar-study/

In life, it's truly how we see ourselves is how others see us. A positive self-image does not come from how we look on the outside, but on how we feel on the inside. To have a lasting, healthy view of self, we must love ourselves first. Thus, the self-love part is also the most important part on your journey to look for a lasting & fulfilling relationship.

The secret sauce for having someone love us truly is WE LOVE OURSELVES unconditionally FIRST. Your partner will never respect you more than you respect yourself. Sometimes it hurts, but it's the truth: You have to love yourself before anyone else can love you.

After my second divorce, I was totally beaten up inside. I spent three whole years alone without dating, but reflecting, healing my wounds, reading books, and searching for meanings; I totally lost confidence in myself. I thought to myself, I crossed two continents to pursue higher education and to seek better career opportunities. Now that I have a master's degree and am working in Fortune 500 companies, I should be proud of my success. But why I am still not happy? Why is my love life so messed up? What's wrong with me?

When I asked my mentor, Peter, he said to me, "Xiaoli, there is nothing wrong with you. You are enough. Happiness is not who you are looking for. It's all about you, find yourself and learn how to accept yourself and love yourself." It was a very abstract concept to me back then. He continued, "If you cannot love yourself, you haven't grasped the meaning of love, so you can't love anyone else." I still remember jotting down his words in my notebook, still confused about how to find myself and love myself.

The journey to finding myself was a totally inner journey. It can be a rather a lonely journey if you let it. I started reading all the books I could find on the subject. Every session with my mentor, he would recommend a new book for me. I would go buy it and finish the book before the next coaching session. Those books were my only true friends during my "dark times." I got to know many different spiritual teachers through their writings.

My transformation did not happen overnight or through some significant incidents, like some people who have a near-death experience or God suddenly speaking to them. I began my transformation by immersing myself in reading books, listening to audio tapes, and going to different workshops. I am a firm believer that repetition will reprogram our conscious mind. I didn't watch TV for years. When driving, I only listened to inspirational CDs, such as Abraham Hicks teachings, Tony Robbins, Brian Tracy, Eckhart Tolle, and many others. Gradually, I found I resonated more with New Age philosophy.

https://en.wikipedia.org/wiki/New_Age

WHAT DOES REALLY LOVE YOURSELF MEAN?

"TO FALL IN LOVE WITH YOURSELF IS THE FIRST SECRET TO HAPPINESS."
– ROBERT MORLEY

To love ourselves means more than just eating healthily, exercising, dressing pretty, reading books, or traveling around the world. We have to look deeper into ourselves.

"The real meaning of love yourself is you don't hide who you really are. You share your feelings and your vulnerability. You own up the truth of your life and your mistakes, you don't need to prove anything to anyone, you don't accept bad treatment or social pressure or feel compelled to do thing you don't want to do. You never worry if you aren't good enough or unworthy and you are at peace with yourself. At the core, its self-respect and self-esteem and believe you are worthy of love" – Gay Hendricks

There are five layers of Self-Love:

1. Physical Well Being: eat well, exercise, enough sleep, take care of our bodies
2. Self-Growth: learning and expanding knowledge. Live life with passion
3. Accepting Who We Are: our backgrounds, our life experience, and our current situation
4. Accept Our Emotions: learn how to express our emotions, whether happy emotions or uncomfortable emotions, find out the reason behind each emotion, and release uncomfortable emotions
5. Love Others and Accept Who They Are

On the journey looking for love, we often expect from our partners what we are not giving ourselves. When we are not providing something for ourselves, we will search for it in those closest to us. If we don't accept ourselves completely, we tend to be critical of our partners about his behaviors. If we have low self-esteem, we tend to be arrogant toward others to feel important. If we don't love ourselves, we will always be looking for signs that our partner doesn't love us. Even when he says, "I love you," you still have doubts that he truly means it.

Almost any relationship problem you may be having is actually a learning to love yourself problem. No one can give you self-love, it has to come from you. Most of us don't know we're suffering from a lack of self-love until we enter a relationship. When you are by yourself, you don't encounter the typical triggers that will indicate a lack of self-love. But a relationship will stir up our deepest needs and fears.

"DO YOU WANT TO MEET THE LOVE OF YOUR LIFE? LOOK IN THE MIRROR" – BYRON KATIE

Accept Our Past Mistakes

The mistake we made in the past certainly makes us believe we were not good enough to be loved.

When Marie came to me, all she wanted to talk about was her past experience. How her parents treated her when she was little, how her ex-husband treated her, and some other abusive relationships. She had been to therapy for years, but her life was still going circles nothing improved or changed. She really wanted to find love and companionship, start a new family with two children, but she felt she couldn't.

We had been working together for quite some time. I realized she was still living with regret and struggling to get over the mistakes she had made in the past. She constantly wished that she could go back and change the decisions that she made. She agonized over the amount of time she had wasted with poor decisions. But she had no motivation to take actions to change!

Everyone makes mistakes. Everyone! If you were to conduct interviews with all the successful people you know, they would fill your notepad with many of the mistakes they made at certain points in their lives. It was not for lack of trying!

The key difference is they did NOT let their mistakes shape their lives forever. Sometimes we may wish to go back in time and erase our mistakes. But life is not that simple. In reality, we cannot delete our mistakes. But take a moment to reflect. If we really take away those mistakes, we actually take away the very experiences that make us unique. Of course, no one wants to sign up for mistakes, but like Tony Robbins said, "Life is always happening for us, not to us." It is really about how we address those mistakes and what we are going to do with that experience to continue to move forward. How can we use these experiences to sculpt our souls, to become more, and to expand our reactions to future events?

The best thing we can do is to begin a new relationship with ourselves. Build a relationship that not only accepts our mistakes but also embraces and loves what those mistakes have given us and made us who we are today.

And if you want more confidence and energy to pursue your dream, instead of wishing that you had done something differently, you must learn to love who you are today. Embrace your mistakes and every part of you.

Unlock Our Core Confidence

Sara felt that no matter what she achieved in her business, she still had not achieved success or was good enough. Interestingly, she is financially wealthy, but she constantly worries that things will fall apart. That is why she feels that she cannot stop achieving.

Michelle is a very attractive lady with a successful career, but she always thinks she is not pretty enough, not the type men will like. Her tendency is once she falls for the men, she would try too hard to please them, ultimately pushing them away.

Jamie is a CFO and highly accomplished businesswoman. She has been looking for the love of her life for years. She tried online dating, matchmaking, and fortune tellers. She tried anything she believed could help her, but she would end up giving up halfway through the process when things started to not go the way she wanted. She would blame coaches, matchmakers, and fortunetellers, claiming they were not very effective. She would even blame the men, claiming all men are bad.

After two divorces, Emily decided to forget about relationships and focus on her children. Once the children had grown up and were out of the house, she began to think about finding a life partner. But she was not confident that she could make the right choice in selecting a partner. She was so afraid that she would get hurt again. She is one of my most loyal Facebook fans, reading my every post and every blog, but she is afraid to take any action.

If these scenarios speak to you, your feelings might be related to a Core Confidence issue.

Often, women tell me they are very confident! But once they receive a rejection in dating or experience a break up in a relationship, they begin to feel self-doubt and start to believe they are not good enough to be in a relationship with a good man. After a few rejections, they tend to give up on finding love altogether.

There are two layers of confidence. One layer is Competency Confidence: Knowledge, Skills, and

Abilities, and another layer is True Confidence or Core Confidence

The First Layer of Confidence is about our competency or personal skills. Examples of this First Layer of Confidence include our job, our social status, the knowledge and training we have in certain areas, or even the hobbies or talents we have developed over years. Because we have gained competency, knowledge, and social status, it will fill us with a sense of confidence. We KNOW we are good at those skills.

However, if we lose one of these things, we can quickly lose the self-confidence that goes along with the First Layer of Confidence. A sudden loss of a job or a demotion in the company will impact our confidence directly. It takes time to build up Competency Confidence, but it can be negatively affected by a single action or event.

I was a career coach for many years. I helped so many men and women in their career transitions. No matter what job titles they had: SVP, CEO, COO, or Director. As soon as they lost their jobs, they started questioning their own ability. They began doubting themselves. Yet, they STILL had the SAME SKILLS to do the job. Sometimes we have been doing these things for so long, we identify only with those external things. Jobs, titles, social status ... once we lose them ... we lose ourselves.

The First Layer of Confidence, in what you do and what you have, can be fleeting. It can easily change with life's circumstances. You can feel confident ... or lost ... depending on external circumstances.

The Second Layer of Confidence is true confidence, or Core Confidence. Core Confidence is the master key to achieving what we want. But it can also unlock our ability to feel happy about what we achieve. It resides deep within us.

Core Confidence is the thing to keep you going when nothing else remains. It's not about a temporary boost we might get from external validation of achievements or relationships with other people. It's the internal validation of knowing and loving who you are. This level of confidence is enduring.

With the Second Layer of Confidence... with Core Confidence ... if your dream guy breaks up with you, you get rejected by someone, or you lose your job right out of the blue, you can still keep going because it doesn't affect who you are. You might get frustrated or begin feeling down, but you are still confident about yourself. You know you will come back better and stronger.

This level of confidence truly makes a secure version of you. So you can create the life you want. Core Confidence really starts with ourselves ... inside!

How do we get that Core Confidence? Through our inner being and through self-love, defining our own values and finding our own worthiness. Learn how to get back in touch with our "inner being." This includes relearning how to love ourselves, trusting our decisions, feeling confident enough to trust others, and be willing to open ourselves up for others to see who we really are.

Once you regain that confidence and "inner being," you will:

- Trust the decisions you make
- Show your more authentic self
- Think more clearly and make the "right" choices
- Quickly know how to identify who is right for you
- Begin to meet the "good ones"

- Stop wasting valuable time on the wrong people
- Not be scared when good things are really happening for you, and
- Start enjoying the company of "good ones" and begin to have fun dating

Ladies, by being your authentic self and true to your "inner being," you will attract the right person to the real you.

Gain Confidence in Dating

My successful love story gained many fans on social media. They were inspired and followed me to get dating and relationship tips. But there is a big problem for them to take the first step. They told me they feel really scared.

Let's take a closer look at Fear:

We all have fear. Everyone can feel afraid of something. My biggest fear back when I was single was of being alone and dying alone. I imaged that after my children went off to college, I was going to be in the house by myself, and I had no one to grow older with. But I used that fear to take action. That's how I decided to do something and not to let that outcome happen!

By definition, fear is an unpleasant emotion caused by the belief that something is likely to cause us pain or hurt. Fear is either from something unknown or from past experience. If we had a bad experience in the past, we will be afraid it might happen again. Likewise, if we never had the experience, our mind creates an anticipated outcome, which may not be entirely accurate, but it scares us nonetheless.

Certainly, dating will stir up or trigger some very uncomfortable feelings, which make us feel fearful. Such as a fear of getting hurt again, fear of being rejected, fear of being vulnerable, or a fear of losing control. All these add up to the biggest fear of all... fear of failure.

Then what do we do? Give up? Run away? Put a shell around ourselves? But how about your dreams and desires? How about happiness? How about enjoying our life to the fullest?

Fear is like a bouncing ball, the harder you push it down, the higher it will bounce back up. The more you resist it, the more fear you will feel. The best practice is to allow yourself to feel those uncomfortable feelings, digest them, understand them, and then release them. Remember, anything you don't release or eliminate, stays with you.

The key here is to learn how to directly look into your fears or uncomfortable feelings and still move through them instead of trying to suppress them. Believe me, a lot of fears are old thoughts and old beliefs. They are not true anymore. They are not true to who you really are.

Releasing fear will create more emotional intimacy for yourself. We all look for intimacy in relationship with our partners. But the first step is to become intimate with ourselves before we can build intimacy with our partners.

What is intimacy? - "into me see" into myself see (myself)

"My willingness to be intimate with my own deep feelings creates the space for intimacy with another." – Shakti Gawain

Only when we create that intimacy with ourselves, when we become comfortable in our own skin, know our own worthiness, our own value... then the confidence will rise to the top – the confidence about who we are!

From that level of confidence in yourself, you will not feel afraid. You will be able to take that first step in dating. You will find worth in yourself. And, you will begin to seek a man worthy of you!

Learn How to Love Yourself

In my coaching, while I am guiding my clients on dating and relationship, I am also embarking on a how to learn self-love journey with them. Here, I will share a few ways for how to learn to love yourself.

1. Write Yourself a Love Letter

Today's mission may make you feel a little vulnerable, but remember that vulnerability is one of the many ingredients for creating love and intimacy.

Imagine that you have received a love letter from the love of your life telling you all the things about you that are lovable, wonderful, and unique.

What are the things you'd want to read?
How would you like to feel?
Think about all of the things you'd want someone to love and honor about you.

Now write that letter to yourself!

Be as loving and generous as you would like your lover to be.

Then put it in an envelope, seal it, and put it in a safe place so that you can open and read it any time you have self-doubts.

2. Make a Commitment to Being Happy

Sometimes, we allow our current (or past) circumstances to determine whether or not we can be happy. However, happiness is both a choice and a state of mind.

What you focus on, expands. Do you know we think between 50,000 to 75,000 thoughts a day? If you focus on one thought negative for 17 seconds, a similar thought will join, and then another similar thought will join. After one minute, you have 3.5 thoughts on something negative, after 5 minutes, you would have 18 similar negative thoughts.

One of the most loving things we can do for ourselves is to affirm the things we want to see more of in our lives. This begins with the words we choose to speak and thoughts about ourselves. The more we focus our time, energy, and attention on the things we want, versus the things we don't want, the more likely we are to attract those things into our life.

The more we focus on the love in and around us, the more love we create. Just as you want to hear how loved you are from your future or present partner, create a habit of telling yourself the things you love and admire about yourself.

The same goes for expressing gratitude. The more time, energy, and attention we give to the things, people, and experiences for which we feel grateful, the more love, happiness, and positive experiences we manifest!

Here are the practical ways how you can make a commitment to being happy,

1. As a way to help you fill your mind with positive and loving thoughts and words, fill a box or jar with positive words, quotes, and phrases. Each morning, pick one and make a commitment to have that be your theme of the day! Or
2. Meditation every morning to set the intention for the day, or
3. Each day write at least three things you feel grateful about life

3. <u>Bring Acceptance to the Way Things Are Now, Knowing They Will Not Always Be This Way</u>

Many times, we look at our current situation and "forevertize" it. We forget that this moment in time, just like the one before it, is temporary. More importantly, we forget that we have the power to change our current circumstances, but ONLY after we bring acceptance to what is currently so.

Usually, what robs us of our happiness has very little to do with our current circumstances. Instead, what causes us to be in fear, sadness, or anxiety over the current situation is that we believe that it "shouldn't" be this way -- that it should be different -- and we make it "wrong." Feel the whole world is against you. See you can feel the strong resistance.

It's impossible to transform anything from the space that it is "bad" or wrong. In order for transformation to take place, acceptance must be present first. Then, and only then, can you clearly see the steps you can take to transform the situation to one that you would prefer to experience.

Bringing acceptance, for example, to the fact that at this moment in your life, you are single, without making this "bad" or "wrong," without beating yourself up, like I am not good enough...etc. When you bring acceptance, then you can clearly see the steps you can take to transform your current relationship status into the one you'd prefer.

Take a few minutes now to think of something that you've been trying to fix or change from the context of it not being the way it "should" be.

Close your eyes and bring acceptance to it by saying,

"I accept that in this moment _____. I bring love and acceptance to this moment and open up to

the possibility that I can transform this situation from a space of love rather than fear."

How did you feel before bringing acceptance to the situation?

How do you feel now that you've brought acceptance to it? What do you see is now possible inside of accepting your current situation?

4. Allow Yourself to Receive Love

Receiving is a form of self-love. When you allow someone else to give you a gift, compliment, their time, their love or attention, you welcome more love into your life!

Many women are really not good at receiving, and I think it just comes down to naturally wanting to give more than we receive. It's really natural for women to want to give to others, but it's often the biggest thing that is holding us back.

Receiving can sometimes make you feel as if you need to do something for the other person in return. You have to deserve it. Ability to receive

The greatest gift you can give someone who is trying to extend their attention, love, or affection is to receive it with an open heart.

If someone gives you a compliment, holds the door for you, offers to help, or wants to pay for something for you, give yourself the gift of receiving by:

1. Allowing yourself to feel the gratitude,
2. Smiling, and
3. Saying, "Thank you!"

5. Set Healthy Boundaries

Are you a people pleaser, find it hard to say "NO" to your partner or people in your life? Do you feel belittled by or unimportant to your partner? Do you avoid conflicts at all costs? Are you afraid to bring up a commitment topic during dating because you are afraid you will scare men away? Do you often suppress your uncomfortable feelings because you don't want to rock the "relationship boat," cause conflicts or arguments, or avoid topics that may lead to a fight? If you said yes to any of them, you might have a boundaries issue

Healthy boundaries aren't just good for your relationship. They're essential.

In fact, it's nearly impossible to have a mature, healthy relationship without boundaries. The problem is that most of us think of walls when we think of boundaries, and that gives the impression of closing yourself off. But that's not really what healthy boundaries do.

People are afraid of setting boundaries because of fear of: a) I will be abandoned or lose the relationship; b) That someone will get hurt or angry with me; c) People won't like me. Or do you feel guilty that making your needs a priority somehow diminishes others or you feel you are "less than" or "not worthy," so making your needs a priority is not an option.

You must learn not to say "yes" when you really want to say "no." Not being honest about your needs forces others to become mind readers. It's unfair to both parties

Deepak Chopra uses a powerful metaphor to describe boundaries in a relationship. He says they're like a screen door. A good screen door will allow a cool breeze to come in while keeping leaves and bugs out. Said another way, well-defined boundaries keep the bad stuff out while still allowing the good stuff into your life.

A healthy and mature relationship needs boundaries. Set limits and boundaries to receive more of what you want. As women, we tend to give and give...but too much giving is tiring, so if we have been giving too much, we tend to blame our partner for unhappiness. ...we need to learn how to set limits and boundaries to receive what we want. As a man experience limits, he is motivated to give more. Because, through respecting limits, he is automatically motivated to question the effectiveness of his behavior patterns, and he will start to make changes. When you learn how to set limits, you learn to relax.

CHAPTER 4 SUMMARY

- A positive self-image does not come from how we look on the outside, but on how we feel on the inside
- The secret sauce for having someone love us truly is WE LOVE OURSELVES unconditionally FIRST

- Your partner will never respect you more than you respect yourself
- The real meaning of loving yourself is you don't hide who you really are. You share your feelings and your vulnerability
- Core Confidence is the thing to keep you going when nothing else remains. It's the internal validation of knowing and loving who you are
- A healthy and mature relationship needs boundaries. When you learn how to set limits, you learn to relax

CHAPTER 4 EXERCISE: SELF-LOVE CHECKLIST

Are you feeling of chronic dissatisfaction no matter what you achieve?

Are you pushing away difficult emotions?

Are you constantly worried about something?

Are you feeling criticized and not feeling accepted?

Are you pleasing people at the expenses of your own peace and wellbeing?

Do you blame others when things go wrong?

Do you feel angry, guilty, or shamed about your past?

Do you like other people to change their behaviors to make you happy?

Did you always attract certain type of partners?

Is it hard for you to forgive other people's mistakes?

Do you believe you will be happy if you find someone who loves you?

If you answer YES to any of these questions. You still have work to do on loving yourself and accepting yourself fully. Go back to 5 ways to love yourself.

CHAPTER 5

MASTER MODERN DATING

"THE FASTEST WAY OF FINDING A SPECIAL PARTNER OR BEING FOUND BY SOMEONE IS TO CREATE POSITIVE DATING EXPERIENCE"
– JOHN GRAY

Modern dating is getting more confusing for a lot of people. Many singles want to find love and a happy relationship, but don't like the dating process. I don't blame them. I have been there and done that too. I hated dating once. I dreamed I could just meet the love of my life one day somewhere in real life just like romantic movies or novels, so I wouldn't have to go through the uncomfortable dating process of meeting many men. But it didn't happen for a long time. It seemed, when we were young, it was so much easier to meet people. But, as we get older, it becomes harder and harder to meet people who fit within our ideal characteristics.

When I complained to my coach Peter, he said to me, "Can you just go out with men to have fun without thinking too much if he is the one for you or not? Practice how to interact with men. The right one will show up, and you will know it." I was thinking why I should waste my time going out with guys if they were not potentials? I resisted his suggestion. Interestingly, now I am giving my clients the same suggestion; "go out to practice and have fun. The right one will show up." Because it works. I found my husband online after I had been out on fifteen dates. He was my sixteenth date. It was the practice with the first fifteen that gave me the skills and confidence to properly interact with the one I wanted to actually be in my life with me.

After one or two bad relationship experiences, we tend to become guarded. We start doubting ourselves. If ONLY we could make the right choices, we would not experience the pain of a bad relationship. Hence, we don't trust ourselves to make the right choice, and we become afraid we might make another mistake.

Some of my clients are women who became single after long marriages or relationships. They are initially overwhelmed by their newly single status and the modern "rules" of dating. They feel frustrated and exhausted because they may have gone on dozens of dates, but still have not met the right man. Or, they've wasted too much time with a man who turned out to be all wrong for them.

Many single women don't know how to talk or connect to the opposite sex, or how to flirt. Not to mention they feel overwhelmed about having to sort through dozens or even hundreds of potential candidates if they are searching using online dating.

These factors keep many women single for too long. They simply give up on dating or don't put in the effort because they don't know how to pick the right guy or mistakenly accept the wrong guy.

Lisa was a VP for a software company and a frequent speaker at business conferences throughout the country. She was a great communicator in her line of work, but when it came to dating, she said she was so shy and nervous that she often didn't know what to say to a man. She felt embarrassed after awkward coffee dates, so she went back to hiding out in her house, fearing to venture out. Here was a woman who was incredibly skilled at talking in front of hundreds of people in a very public setting. But she could not get past the first few lines of talking to a man in a personal setting.

Kristine tried online dating for the first time and ended up meeting a man who lived 400 miles away. She spent a month speaking to him on the phone. She told me she had found her soulmate and the man wanted to marry her. She decided to be exclusive with him, even though they had not met, because he sent flowers and gifts and called her every single day. When I asked her how she could fall in love with a man she had never met in person, and so quickly, too, she said it was because she was so attracted to what the man said to her. It had been years since anyone had spoken to her in such a way. "I had not been dating for years; I guess I lost my judgment, had no clue what was going on. He made lots of promises," she said.

After getting divorced, Mina entered into a relationship with a man she met on a business trip. In her heart, she knew the man wasn't the right one in many ways, but she stayed in the relationship for five years because she felt empty and lonely without him. She was afraid she might not be able to meet another guy better than him. The longer she stayed in this go-nowhere relationship, the harder it was to break up. Finally, she did, but it created a lot of emotional baggage. She blamed herself for staying in that wrong relationship for so long, not only wasting her time, but also destroying her self-esteem in the process.

Why Dating?

In a relationship, experience is your teacher. Dating is to experiment with what you want and what you don't want. Many times, you might not know what you want until you find out what you don't want in the process of dating.

Julia started online dating. She lives in Los Angeles but talked to guys everywhere, such as Chicago, Hawaii, and New York City. She was consistently on Skype or Facetime but had not really experienced a live face-to-face date in many months. She "dated" a guy in Boston for about a year, yet they only met 4 times in person. Finally, giving in to the exhaustion of the effort to stay in contact, and frustrated with the different friendship circles, the tiring work and travel schedule, and the three-hour time zone difference, she had the courage to leave the relationship. She came to tell me, "I thought I was into the long-distance relationship thing. When we got together, there was lots of excitement and passion. But we also had space to do our own thing. But in reality, it's very tiring, even when you're trying to have a conversation on Skype. I am done with this long-distance thing."

Like Amy, in my earlier example, Lily had never been married and had no children of her own. But she did not mind dating men with children. After a few dates with a man who had three children, with diaper and baby stuff everywhere in his house. She started questioning herself if she would be okay to deal with all the mess and be a stepmother for three children, considering she had never had children yet.

Dating is a sorting process. Learning from mistakes. Dating is also a process to see if you are compatible with each other. Good Chemistry is just the starting point at the beginning of the relationship. To have a long-lasting happy relationship, compatibility is the key. Compatible on values, lifestyle, interests in day-to-day life. Too many women put initial chemistry as a priority but realize later on in the relationship that many other things are not compatible. Some stayed in the relationship just because they were afraid they might not be able to find someone better.

If you want to learn how to date, Dr. John Gray's "Mars and Venus on a Date" is a great resource for you to learn dating skills and how to find out who is right for you.

Why Dating Is So Challenging and Daunting

Dating has become very challenging and daunting for many women. Here are some of the basic reasons:

- **Lack of Clarity**

  If you are not clear on what exactly you are looking for, you waste lots of time on the wrong people. In asking many women what they want from relationship, most of them couldn't articulate their inner-most needs, but more focus on the potential partner's attributes, the look, height, job, income, and social status, or looking for someone to spend time with, go out for fun or travel with, but once they get that person who meets their criteria, they still feel something is missing. They are not totally happy.

If you want to date effectively, it's important to know your outcome before you rush yourself to go on dates. Begin with the end in mind and know exactly what success looks like for you. That's why I spend a solid 60 to 90 minutes on the first session with clients to define their success pictures. If you have wishy-washy goals, you only attract wishy-washy people.

What success looks like to you is only based on your own experience and preference; it's unique to you. What's the purpose of dating? What are the must haves? What qualities and characters are you looking for that you know would make you happy? What are the deal breakers? It's very important to take some time to develop a clear picture before you started dating.

Because the clarity helps you to realize sooner that you are with the wrong person. It makes it easier for you to move on to finding the right person. The sooner you discover that a person is not right for you, the sooner you can move on and find the right person.

- **Afraid to Rock the Boat**

The reason there are so many unsatisfied, unhappy women dating is that they are afraid to be bold about what they want. They are afraid to rock the boat or afraid to sound too demanding to the men.

Ada had been dating a man, Ken, for some time. Things went very well in the beginning. She was initially happy. Finally, she had found someone who connected with her on so many levels. Because he was such a good catch, she was very cautious not to ask too many questions. At the six-month mark, the guy started talking and planning a future with her and suggested they moved in together. He wanted them to spend more quality time together and continue growing and knowing each other in their daily life. Ada was excited and started talking about having family and talked about having children with him. Her boyfriend suddenly said, "I want to be a family with you, but I do not want children. I want it to be just us. I never wanted to have children." Ada could feel her heart sinking. She really dreamed of being a mother. She was tortured between this relationship with Ken and her dream to be a mother. If she had communicated early on in this relationship the importance of motherhood, she could have avoided stepping into this relationship with her whole heart and may have avoided a significant heartbreak when she chose motherhood over Ken.

Jane has health issues when she eats certain foods. For example, she needs to avoid sugar and gluten because her body experiences negative reactions when she eats them. But she is afraid if she states this on her first date with a man, it might scare her date away. So she tends to go on many dates, eating deserts or pizza that her date orders for her. When the date is over and she goes home, she feels bad from the effects of the food she should have avoided in the first place. She did not have the courage to say, "No, I cannot eat those types of food. Can we order something else instead?" Going out to eat with her dates became very stressful for her.

Being bold does not mean you must demand or aggressively express what you want or must have. It does not have to be a "my way or the highway" moment. It is really how you communicate your needs and desires. Being bold takes confidence. Playing down your needs or lowering your standards to please your date will never take you on the right path in connecting you with your Mr. Right. It can only make the process of dating feel daunting for you. You cannot enjoy the moment because you are not speaking and acting from your heart. Good quality men who are out there searching for women will not be intimidated by you speaking up and saying what you want. Quite the contrary, your confidence and your boldness will be a very attractive quality to him. The question is;

are you willing to step up and say what you want?

- **<u>You Are Doing Too Much in Dating</u>**

   If you feel dating is exhausting, the problem could be that you are trying too hard. In dating, sometimes you need to do less. I know it's a challenging concept, especially if you're a go-getter. You like to get things done, you want to achieve results. Your go-getter mentality will give you success in business, but not in dating.

   As we talked about how to dance between your masculine and feminine energy, it is a perfect opportunity to practice your feminine energy while dating. You are being receptive and letting men chase you and please you. Watch their actions.

   That means:

   o   Do not find any excuses to text him if he hasn't texted you for a few days

- o Do not panic if he pulls away, chasing him and asking him why he is avoiding
- o Do not immediately begin doing things for him, like cooking, doing laundry, or bringing takeout food
- o Do not plan dates

Your job is to be receptive, observe what kind of effort he makes to see you and respond accordingly. If a guy is not excited to see you, with him taking action and planning dates during the first month, it is a clear sign your relationship is probably not going too far.

If you clearly know what you want, have the confidence to express what you want, and stay in your feminine energy, suddenly, dating will begin to feel good again, more relaxed, more fun. You don't have to constantly figure out what the next step is – because you're allowing yourself to be pursued instead of doing the pursuing.

Doing nothing is hard because you like to take action. But sometimes, you must let a man reveal himself through his actions. In the process of doing nothing, by letting men pursue you, it might trigger uncomfortable feelings for you. You may feel you might not find someone like him. Or, you may fear being rejected and be concerned about how that may impact your self-image. You may even begin to start blaming yourself as being too old, not pretty enough, or not slim enough.

When you meet people in real life, either through online applications or through matchmaking, you still need to date to find out if you are compatible. Some women have this fantasy that their prince charming will just appear out of thin air, sweep them off their feet, get married and happily ever after. I can assure you that even if prince charming just happens to knock your door, he will probably still want to date you to see if you are the right woman for him. You cannot escape the dating process.

Learn How to Flirt

When I use the word "flirt," some people might associate it with a negative image. It sometimes manifests into an image of women making straightforward sexual advances toward men while on a date. This is NOT the flirting that I mean when I use the term "The Art of Flirting." What I want to focus on is the attitude, the energy, and the mindset behind flirting.

Once, I went to John Gray's relationship workshop, he used an analogy to describe flirting. I really like it. What do you do when you go shopping? When you go shopping, you walk around the store and look at all the products. You have fun checking out what you like and what you don't like. You have no need to prove yourself to the salesperson about what you should buy or why. You freely try things out, without judgment.

This is the perfect mindset and attitude when you go on a date. And it is the perfect and positive energy you should use when flirting. Flirting energy says, "I am looking and liking what I see. I would like to get to know more about you." This flirting energy is very exciting to men because it compliments their ability to make you happy. A man is always looking for the opportunity to please you, especially if he is interested in you.

Dating became so stressful and nerve-racking for people because for high achieving professionals, they treat the event like a business project with hard deadlines. They are busy. Time is extremely important. They do not want to waste time. Therefore, they go on dates to hunt the ONE and attempt to instantly decide on the first date if he is the ONE and worthy of their time. For both people on the date, it is IMPOSSIBLE to relax. Your mind is constantly judging the person across the table. You are on the date physically, but you are not mentally engaged in the conversation. Trust me, the person sitting across the table can sense this.

Don't go into a date worried about what comes next. Dating is all about fun and enjoyment. Keep it light. Focus on learning about the other individual and making a new friend. When you hold this perspective in your mind, it takes lots of pressure off your shoulders. A great friendship is the foundation for a great relationship.

Don't rush to judgment about whether you like him or not, or what he is thinking about you. When you attempt to instantaneously judge, your mind is not focused on the person who is sitting across from you. Set judgment aside on the first date and try to relax. Listen to what is actually being said. Take your time. Stay in the present moment. Really genuinely get to know this person.

Remember, as a woman, your job is NOT to impress. Your job is to maintain a place of openness...sending the energy, "I am open to finding out if I like you. If you are the one for me, then show it and impress me." Always let the man be the one to impress you.

Online Dating

Many people experience frustration through online dating. They start with hope and excitement but come out frustrated, burned out, and even broken-hearted. "Online dating is so confusing!" I hear this from my clients all the time, and it is also what I discovered when I went back into the world of dating after my marriage ended in divorce.

I had heard about online dating, of course, but I thought that only losers and players hung out there. I was also a mom and had a successful career. I didn't want anyone to know that I was on a dating website! Not only would that be embarrassing, but I was also way too busy to waste my time chatting online or going on countless dates with the wrong people.

But then again, I wasn't so young anymore either, and I didn't want to go to bars or nightclubs to meet a man. It felt as though online dating websites were my only option. I decided to give it a try. And guess what happened? I met my husband, Jim, on a dating website, and we are now happily married.

BUT I did not have overnight success.

When I first started online dating, I felt so overwhelmed. The first issue I encountered was that there are many dating websites out there. I had no idea which one to choose, and this was so confusing for me. Then once I had chosen a website, I didn't know what to say, how to act, how to interact. Even the technology was scary and overwhelming: setting up profiles, posting photos, texting and messaging. I got a few messages, and even a few dates, but I either ended up texting with what I can only call a "pen pal" (this is NOT what I wanted) or wasting time on dates with people I just did not connect with. A few times, I thought I had finally connected with someone, then suddenly he pulled away without a trace.

All of this left me feeling very disheartened and disappointed. I felt like quitting.

I am sure if you have tried online dating, you have probably had some similar experience.

Online dating takes some strategy and skills.

Elements of a Successful Online Dating

★ Set a Healthy Mindset for Online Dating

This is the most important aspect of online dating. Before you decided to do online dating, I would really encourage you to have the right mindset about it. If you truly don't feel good about it, then don't do it. The worst situation is that you hate online dating, but you still do it. It will not bring any good results for you. You can't hate something and expect good in return.

When women join my coaching program to find love, I never push them to go for online dating. We always start working on relationship patterns, how to tap into and stay in feminine energy, how to release old emotions, how to understand men's psychology, and how to set the right mindset about dating. Interestingly, most of them feel excited again to go out dating and are willing to try online dating. Remember, any success is only 20% mechanical. 80% is our mindset.

Statistics show that the total number of single people in the U.S. is currently 54 million, while the total number of people who have tried online dating is 49 million. That's a pretty huge crossover. In 2017 alone, 19% of brides said they met their spouse online, 17% through friends, 15% during college, and 12% from work. Again, online dating is the clear leader. Whether you like it or not, online dating sites and apps have become a major part of single life, and they are not going away anytime soon.

In reality, it's hard to meet someone these days. We have our small lives: our circle of married friends, our coworkers, a few single people. As you get into your late 30s or early 40s, the bar scene really gets worn out. While it is nice to say I want to meet someone organically, where our eyes meet, so I can feel that chemistry that does not happen very often. This is why I believe in online dating. It creates an opportunity to meet people you couldn't possibly meet in real life. Of course, you may meet some players, liars, and flakes. But those people also exist offline as well. The key here is to learn how to weed those people out.

It matters how you master online dating game.

✶ Choose Proper Dating Apps

There are over 2,500 dating apps just in the US, and it's still growing. Estimates put there to be 8,000 dating websites worldwide, each offering advantages and disadvantages. Just by hearing those numbers, you probably already feel overwhelmed.

The common question is which one is the best? If people decided to spend money and time on this, it's normal we want to go for the best.

The truth really is that there is no best website. It's all about which dating website fits your needs based on your demographic area, your age bracket, and your budget. Each website has its own focus and uniqueness. For example,

Tinder is a location-based social discovery application that facilitates communication between mutually interested users. You can use Tinder without Facebook. The key is having good photos. You have to put your absolute best foot forward. Put up between 3 and 5 pictures. You also need one or two sentences that encapsulates what you are looking for - if you are looking for intelligent, educated men, you have to say that up front. Tinder is all about the visual - so the visual has to be strong. The written part of the profile will help to draw in (or select out) the right matches, but it is not an exact science, of course.

Bumble puts women in charge – Similar to Tinder, but after both parties have 'liked' each other, the woman has 24 hours to send a message. The woman has to send the message first, then the man can communicate with her. You can write a short profile, free of charge. It can also be used without Facebook if preferred.

Our Time: Exclusively for singles aged 50 and up who are looking for deep relationships with other older singles. The site features an easy, sign up process, as well as an impressive set of search features for its users. Very user-friendly, providing a ton of helpful features for its mature user base.

If your culture is important to you, if your religion is important to you, and you want to find other people that are like you or like-minded, you should go to niche sites. Like Christian mingles for Christian people looking for like-minded, Two Red Bean is for people who want to date Asian only.

So the question is how to pick the dating website that fits your needs. I have a client who told me that she didn't get many results on Match.com, but was doing amazing on Plenty of Fish because she is over 60.

Generally, it's good to start on a big-name brand site that has a decent reputation. Best practice is to have two dating websites going at the same time.

You can choose one big brand website and one focus website or niche website. While the big site has more prospective candidates from which to choose, you will also have more competition and more weeding out of the less desirable suitors. Likewise, the niche site will have a smaller pool of potential candidates, but less competition.

✱ **Write an Authentic Dating Profile**

Many people rush into online dating without spending time on their dating profile. That's why you may have seen so many generic profiles that look the same. I met some people who are a really good catch in real life, but their overly generic profiles made them hard to get noticed online.

I really took the time to craft my profile and also asked my writer friend to do some editing for me. A dating profile needs to be unique, authentic, and represent who you are. This is the first impression you make. Don't take it lightly. You spend time creating a unique professional profile for your LinkedIn account. Why not do the same for your personal dating profile?

This part is the most difficult part for most people. Some of my clients said they have writer's block. They become unsure of what to say on their profile.

There is a great book called "The Catch Your Match Formula" by Dave Elliott, which guides you on how to write an authentic online profile. I used some of his formulas to help my clients with crafting their dating profiles. It can be accomplished in one day if you set your mind to it.

★ Effective Online Communication

This is the most delicate part of online dating. Many of my conversations went nowhere. You are excited about the guy who wrote to you, but after a few messages exchanged back and forth, they go dark. Or maybe you wrote to someone you thought might be perfect for you, but he never replied back.

This part can cause some women to feel discouraged, feel a sense of rejection. It is easy for some women would take it personally, and to start doubting themselves. Once again, triggering those limiting beliefs like, "I am not good enough" or "I am not likable" or "I am too old for online dating."

The only way to solve this problem is to be persistent. Online dating can be a numbers game. If you meet enough people, you can find your Mr. Right. Match.com did an analysis of their website showing, statistically, that each person averages between twelve to thirteen people before you will meet someone you connected with and has the potential for a relationship. I dated sixteen people to meet my love. I know one lady who dated 45 people. One of my friends met her husband after meeting two men online. It varies!

The purpose of all of this online communication is to simply see if you two want to meet in person. So don't stay too long at this stage of communication. Usually, after two or three emails, I would suggest you ask for a phone conversation if the man has not already suggested it. I always believe the voice is energy. By talking to a person over the phone, you can pretty much predict if the real conversation will be pleasant or not.

In order to make online communication achieve the purpose for you to meet people in real life, it's important to keep it short, precise but fun. Humor never goes wrong in the communication process and tends to get attention from the other side. This is my most favorite part of online dating. I also guide my clients on how to communicate in a fun and light way. Nothing should be too serious at this stage.

If you are not good at online communication, don't worry. Everything takes practice to become good at it. Some women fear they might miss out someone great online if they haven't written proper content. Online dating is a platform for you to practice. Don't be afraid to make mistakes. If the right partner shows up, nothing is a mistake.

Meet People in Real Life

Of course, online dating is not the only option to find love. Certainly, you can meet your man in real life. The only thing stopping you is when you don't leave the house, or you don't step outside of your comfort zone.

We all have busy schedules and many obligations in life. The art is how to incorporate meeting your potential mate into your busy schedule. One way you can do it is to make a social calendar, making sure you schedule one or two social events per week in advance on your calendar.

There are many places you can meet men in real life, literally everywhere... Here are a few suggestions:

1. Coffee shops: Nowadays, lots of business people have small meetings in coffee shops.

   You can read books (e.g. a romantic book) with a cup of coffee. If the weather is good, you could sit outside, enjoy the sunshine while reading the story. Surprisingly, people might start talking to you.

2. BBQ Parties: Go to friends or family weekend parties. Or, better yet, host one yourself. Ask people to bring food to share... potluck style. But more importantly, ask people to bring their friends so you can meet new people.

3. Check out events on Facebook: If your friends on Facebook are also going, message them, so you can meet them at the event.

4. Networking: Find events to attend or go to happy hours after work. Some events are more business oriented, but it is still networking... and you will meet like-minded people.

5. Volunteer: Make time to help at a charity event. Find your passion and spend time doing it.

6. If you are a business owner, the local chamber of commerce is a great place to meet people. They always host a lot of events.

7. High-end Health clubs: If you enjoy working out, the high-end health clubs

usually have a café. Spend time after your workout sitting down and relaxing at the café. There are also clubs that host fitness workshops, make a time to attend.

8. Meetup groups: Log onto Meetup and find a group of people who have similar interests and tastes for activities. Go Meet Up and talk.

The biggest challenge for people is how to strike up a conversation and show your interest.

1. Make sure the event or activity is something that excites you. If you have a passion for it and if it is something you love, you will be more talkative and social. Do NOT go just for the sake of meeting people.

2. Once you are at the event, it is very important to stay relaxed. Take notice of the little things. Be observant of the people around you and pick out what you like about them. Observe and appreciate others. Love starts with appreciation. Be interested, be curious.

3. When you are present, relaxed, and soft, your energy will attract masculine men

who will make a point to come and talk to you. Remain relaxed and soft when they do.

Matchmaking

Many busy professionals start seeking a matchmaker to find suitable candidates. That's another option. Matchmaking has its own pros and cons. On one side, you can certainly save tons of time by not having to browse people online or taking time to get out to meet people. You can meet people based on your criteria in terms of age range, education, occupation, location. The drawback is that you can only meet a limited number of people, and chemistry is not something a matchmaker can guarantee. If you have a good matchmaker, make sure she/he will also screen for you on your potential match's emotional background, that he is totally emotionally available. A few of my clients have told me that they had been on the matchmaking journey. But some of the men they met through this process were still focused in the past, constantly talking about ex-spouses or ex-girlfriends. It was a huge failure in their eyes.

One thing to keep in mind is that no matter how you meet people — online, in real life, or through matchmaking — you need to go through the dating process to get to know each other. Some clients met good quality potentials through matchmaking but could not keep them interested in the relationship. Mastering communication during modern dating is critical.

Why Men Pull Away

It happens a lot in today's dating world that some men will pull away as soon as you start falling for him. Here are some reasons

✶ You've built them up in your head before you've gotten to know them.

When you have things in common, and suddenly it hits you, "Wow, this person could be someone I really like!" What you are doing is focusing on those few qualities or interests that are like your own and making those the focal point of attraction.

Instead of taking time to get to know them, you build them up in your head, and you fall for the idea of who this person could be for you, instead of who he actually is.

Vera met a guy online, and before they had even met, she already felt that he was the love she'd been looking for. She became excited and nervous. She spent hours texting with him and became so available whenever he wanted to talk. Guess what? The guy never asked her out, but continued to only text her. Finally, he faded away, left her sad and heartbroken.

It's important to not put someone on a pedestal, because the moment you do that, you go from attraction to admiration and feel that you need to earn their love and affection. When, in reality, all you have to do is be yourself.

The moment you classify this guy as someone perfect for you, you devalue yourself; thinking it's you who needs to prove you deserve them. What you should be trying to do is prove if this person is compatible for you and if you'd be a good match that compliments each other.

✶ <u>**You lower your standards after you've fallen.**</u>

The tendency for some women is that when they like someone, they start to lower their standards. They accept their wrong behaviors and hope to change these wrong behaviors in the future.

When you try too hard to please someone or change who you are and the things you value, you not only lose their respect, but you suddenly become less attractive to them. I'm not saying play hard to get, but walk into every relationship with your values and standards intact to who you truly are. Learn how to set healthy boundaries throughout the relationship.

✶ <u>**You rush the relationship.**</u>

Sometimes, when we want something so badly, we push to have it quickly. But any relationship of quality takes time to achieve. Men want to pursue and not to be pursued. When you rush, you emasculate men, they can't step up to be a producer. He will either shut down or pull away from you.

If you want a healthy relationship, let things progress naturally. Men can feel when you are trying too hard. Take things slowly. Do not try and control the outcome.

✳ <u>You accept the wrong people</u>.

Some women are so desperate to find love, they are afraid they might not find someone better, so they will accept the wrong people and become stuck in an unhappy relationship wondering why this is not working AGAIN.

It isn't the wrong person who is the problem, the problem is in choosing that wrong person.

In dating, when men tell you, "I'm not ready for a relationship" or "I'm very into my career right now." You must believe it. Do not hope they will change this perspective for you. You need to learn how to build the self-confidence to walk away from the people who are not right for you. Dating is truly about taking a hard look at ourselves and realizing the problem might not be them, but there are areas within ourselves where we need to improve.

CHAPTER 5 SUMMARY

- In a relationship, experience is your teacher. Dating is an experiment to discover what you want and what you don't want.
- Many times, you might not know what you want until you find out what you don't want in the process of dating.
- You must allow yourself to be pursued instead of doing the pursuing.
- Online dating creates an opportunity to meet people you couldn't possibly meet in real life.
- You can meet your man in real life. The only thing stopping you is when you don't leave the house or you don't step outside of your comfort zone.

CHAPTER 5 EXERCISE: PRE-DATING

Don't rush into dating. Before you start dating, take some time to answer the following questions. These will give you much clarity on what type of relationship and partner you are looking for and identify who you are and what values you can bring into the relationship.

1. Who are you? How do you show up on a regular basis? What is your identity?

2. Who do you to be? In your heart of hearts, what do you aspire to be, do, or have? What do you stand for? What do you want to create? What do you want your life to look like? What kind of relationship vision do you see yourself enjoying?

3. What is your mission? Clarity comes with power. What is it that makes you feel great? What lights you up and makes you feel satisfied? Think of the last time you felt really joyful or on purpose. What were you doing? If you could accomplish anything in your life, what would it be and why?

4. What can your partner expect from you? What are the benefits and features you offer a partner? Why are you a great catch? What's special or unique about you and sets you apart from the crowd?

5. How do you want you to be perceived? Begin with the end in mind. What do

potential prospects likely think of you? What's the common compliment you receive from others, whether they have known you for a long time or just met you? Is there something that needs to be addressed?

6. What is it that you don't really like about yourself or feel could be a liability when it comes to attracting your love?

7. What's your dating purpose? What are the must haves?

8. About the One: What age range are you comfortable with when choosing your one? How far are you willing to travel to meet your One? Do you have a preference of career for your One? Salary range? Fitness level, saver or spender, political view, love children vs hates children, drinker vs non-drinker, smoker vs non-smoker, drug user vs no drugs, religious view, special hobbies, travel preference, open to relocating, and anything else you can think of

9. What's the number one benefit you offer a potential partner?

If you could only be known for one thing that you bring to the table for a potential partner, what do you want it to be? What's the most compelling offer you can make that would make the right person for you sit up and take notice immediately?

10. What is it about you and you only that sets you apart from everyone else?

What's the first thought that people who know you well associate with you and you only? What is the one comment you hear about yourself from others over and over again?

11. What do people like and value about you the most?

What's the most common compliment you receive from others, whether they've known you for a long time or just met you? What do people like and admire about you the most?

CHAPTER 6

THE HAPPINESS CODE

7 PROVEN STEPS TO ATTRACT TRUE LOVE

Here comes the action part of the book. From my own journey to find love and the journeys of many other women I helped, there are 7 time-proven steps you can take to attract true love and build the happy, lasting relationship you desire.

1. Love yourself and Feel Sexy in Your Own Skin

You are a good catch, both worthy and lovable. If you can be authentic about who you are, you will attract the right person to the *real* you. The secret to having long-lasting love is not playing the "hard to get" game or bending over backward to please to your partner in the hope that it will make him happy. Those actions will backfire and work against your end goal. As women, we have this natural energy to connect to a man's heart by leveraging our feminine energy.

Masculine men are compelled by feminine energy. However, this powerful energy tends to be buried under our busy demanding lives with so many things to manage, control, and achieve. The sources of this authentic power are within you, just waiting to be awakened and unleashed.

You can feel "Sexy in Your Own Skin" by tapping into the natural feminine energy inside you. This will help you to be authentic about who you are and attract the right person into your life. Once you master this piece, you will go through your daily activities, and great men will be attracted to you like a magnet.

2. Put the Past Behind You

I want you to know that you CAN "Restore Your Inner Confidence" if you have been hurt in the past.

This seems to be the most difficult task for most people. Some people live in resentment and depression for years. Bad experiences tend to cloud our judgment about ourselves and about others.

After one or two bad relationships, we lose confidence in ourselves and begin to not trust our decisions on finding love anymore.

The fear of being hurt again can make us feel paralyzed and prevent us from making decisions or taking any action.

The fastest way to detach from your past and move on is to work with a relationship coaching or therapist. They can provide special techniques and strategies that can help you release and heal your emotional wounds, so that you can move forward and meet someone who will make you happy.

3. Set an Intention on what You Want for Your Next Relationship

After we put the past behind us, it's a perfect opportunity to set your intention for what MUST be in your next relationship.

You can set your intentions through this exercise:

Begin with the end in mind and know exactly what your ideal relationship looks like for you. Clearly defining these "MUST HAVES" is crucial.

- What's the purpose of the relationship?
- What are your values?
- What qualities and characteristics are you looking for in the relationship that you know will make you happy?
- And, on the opposite end of the spectrum, what are the "Deal Breakers?"

Pay attention to how you want to *feel* about yourself and how you want to be treated in a relationship. It's very important to take some time to develop a clear picture before you step into your love adventure.

With clarity, you will meet potential partners and quickly realize at the very beginning if he is not the right man for you. This will make it easier for you to stop spending time with the wrong person and quickly move on to finding the right person.

Reverse Engineering Exercise

If you are not really sure what you want from your next relationship, think about past relationships.

- What things or actions did you not like in your past relationship?
- What opposite action would have potentially made you happy?

These are the natural steps to defining the "MUST HAVES" and will be the foundation for the Intention of your next relationship.

I see many people go out on dates with wishy-washy intentions. This will only attract wishy-washy people into your life.

Many people feel dating is daunting and draining mainly because they are not very clear on what they want in a relationship.

The key here is to focus on what kind of relationship you want, not what type of man you are seeking.

Having fixed ideals about what type of man you seek will limit your options. It will restrict your efforts. This is one of the many reasons why women complain that there are no good, quality men out there in the dating world.

The problem is not that the dating world lacks quality people. (There are plenty of quality people out there, just like you!) The main reason is we don't know exactly what we are looking for in a relationship.

Focusing on the attributes of the man will result in you wasting time with the wrong people. The unfortunate effect is that you could easily pass up on a great potential partner, just because he is not on your "ideal man" list: looks, age, occupation, social status, hobbies, etc.

4. Understand Man Code

If past relationships gave you lots of confusion about your partner's behavior, now is a great opportunity to understand men on a deep level.

Men long for love and a meaningful relationship as much as women do.

Our failed past relationships are not all about men being players, cheats, or liars. It's mainly because *men and women have different values, emotional needs, motives, and communication style.* Once you master understanding men, you will be ready when the next man shows up in your life. You will feel confident and comfortable to interact with them and truly build intimacy with the man you love, because you will understand them.

Interestingly, some women come to me after a divorce or break up and ask me if I can match them with a quality man. I always tell them that finding a new man will not solve the problem. They need to understand why the relationship wasn't working in the first place to clearly see the fundamental reasons that resulted in the divorce or breakup.

Some women used a matchmaker to be paired up with high-quality men, but had to come back for more coaching because they did not understand the man?

Matchmaking will not work if you don't have the foundation to understand the difference between women and men.

You can refer to Chapter 3 and Chapter 5 to understand men and how to interact with men in dating and in a relationship. Dr. John Gray's book, *Men from Mars and Women from Venus* is a great book to start with to understand the difference between men and women.

https://www.marsvenus.com/john-gray-mars-venus.htm

Alison Armstrong is another my favorite expert on understanding men with amazing workshops and online programs

http://www.understandmen.com/

5. Practice Your Relationship Skills Through Dating

Loving yourself (for who you are) and "Tapping into Your Feminine Energy" is all about BEING. How you should behave and act to have the love you want.

Now is the action part. Here's how to practice loving your sexy self AND putting your feminine energy into your modern dating life.

Remember, dating is only a sorting process: a chance to practice techniques, learn from mistakes and emphasize or reinforce the successes.

In building a relationship, experience is your teacher. And it will help you to find and recognize partners who can fulfill your needs for increased intimacy, good communication, and a great love life. We need to learn, practice, and update our dating skills.

Learn how to weed out those people who are not compatible or suitable for you...quickly!

Let the dating process unfold in front of you and enjoy the moment in time. Many people treat dating like projects with deadlines. They go on dates to hunt for the ONE and wish to decide on the first date if he is the ONE.

It is IMPOSSIBLE to relax on these kinds of dates, and the man will sense it right away. Your mind is constantly judging the person across the table. Some ladies want to find love so badly, they go on dates every day of the week. Eventually, they run out of energy, get dejected, and give up on dating altogether. The stress and frantic pace was their enemy.

Dating is an opportunity to gain experience to find out what you like and don't like.

It's a great opportunity to practice how you interact with men.

6. Nourish Your Life Outside the Relationship

Everyone has a special passion, interest, or talent. I have never met a single person who didn't have something they are passionate about or good at. When they talk about their passion, their eyes sparkle.

As women, when we are especially attracted to a man, we get blinders. Suddenly, everything we used to love before gets pushed to the side. In order to counteract your urge to go into "doing" mode for him, you need to make it a point to experience as much of your feeling self as you can. Anything that puts you in touch with your sensual self, such as dance classes, massages, spending time in nature, even taking a long bath.

When you make yourself the priority and commit yourself to your passions, he'll know he has found a woman he can love forever.

When was your last time you worked on your hobby or your favorite project? Has it been sitting idle or neglected? Do certain activities make your heart sing? Did you know you are the most charming and attractive when you talk about your passion?

Men will be attracted to and fall in love with you just by hearing that spark in your voice.

You have no idea how beautiful you are when you are talking about something you care for and are passionate about. It is a huge turn on for men. Learn how to use this attribute to engage and excite your partner.

7. Make a Daily Gratitude Check-Up

It is normal to feel frustrated when we do not feel loved, or when the things we desire most are not coming to fruition. This frustration blinds us to the many amazing things happening in our life right now for which we should be thankful.

When I think back on my life, everything was progressing for the better, even if I didn't feel it at the time.

I believe you will find that things happen for a reason. Using the "one door closes, another door opens" mentality will help you through the rough patches. This Daily Gratitude Check-Up reinforces this positive outlook. A positive mental attitude is more attractive to the opposite sex than a negative mental attitude.

Take time, starting TODAY, to identify what you feel grateful about in your life. Make it a daily habit. Eventually, better things will come your way when you are thankful for what you already have.

Here is a daily check-up exercise you can use as a reference:

<u>BEFORE I START MY DAY:</u>

How do I feel?
I want to let go of _____

I am most grateful for _____

Self-care: The more I take care of myself, the happier I will be. When I'm happy, I bring happiness to the world.

I commit to 1-3 things on the self-care list. Include time and activities.

My intention for TODAY:

What do I want to focus on today? Include time and activities.

What activities do I need to do today to make my life better? Include time and end goal.

BEFORE BED

My biggest celebration of the day was _____

Today, I learned _____

I acknowledge myself for _____

CONCLUSION

A loving, committed, soulmate life-partnership IS for everyone – including you. But you need to take action. If you think, "If it's meant to be, it will just happen," Then that thought is passive and will keep you single for a long time.

What holds back most smart and conscious women that I meet is that they feel they don't have the clarity and support they need to succeed. Therefore, they stay resigned and unwilling to take the risk to open up for possibilities and stand for their greatest vision in love.

If you follow these 7 steps and take the time to try out the exercises, even if only ONE of them is right for you, you will find yourself on the path to finding true love faster, and you will increase your confidence in having a long-term committed relationship with the RIGHT man. Success in love is like success in any other area of your life. It takes commitment, intention, investment, work, and getting out of your comfort zone.

If you feel it's hard to do all these steps on your own, I've discovered the most powerful, fastest, and most efficient tools, practices, and strategies to help you.

Mastering love is no harder than learning how to ride a bike. Sure, the first five minutes *is scary* because you wobble and falter, and you fear falling and hitting the ground hard. But if you have training wheels, you CAN'T fall. If you have someone running beside you, you WON'T fail. If you know that pretty much everyone who's learned to balance and learned to peddle has succeeded before you, you can stay the course because you know you CAN'T fail.

That's what it's like to master love. I know you can do it if you apply yourself. And it's my intention to make it THAT easy for you to succeed. I am very passionate about helping you to make the journey for you to live your dream, so you can succeed in love as much as you've already succeeded in your career and other areas of your life. Let's begin that conscious journey to lasting love with the very first step together.

APPENDIX

HERE ARE TOP 15 BOOKS THAT HELPED ME TRANSFORMED TREMENDOUSLY ON MY JOURNEY TO LOVE

James Allen, "As a Man Thinketh"

Brene Brown, "The Gifts of Imperfection"

Rhonda Byrne, "The Secret"

Gary Chapman, "The 5 Love Languages"

Deepak Chopra, "The Path to Love"

Dr. Wayne Dyer, "The Power of Intention"

Arielle Ford, "The Soulmate Secret"

John Gray, "Men from Mars and Women from Venus"

Ester and Jerry Hicks, "Ask and It Is Given"

Ester and Jerry Hicks, "The Law of Attraction"

Napoleon Hill, "Think and Grow Rich"

Sharon L. Lechter and Greg S. Reid, "Three Feet from Gold"

David Richo, "How to Be an Adult in Relationships"

Eckhart Tolle, "The Power of Now"

Eckhart Tolle, "A New Earth – Awakening to Your Life's Purpose"

ABOUT THE AUTHOR

Xiaoli Mei is a certified Relationship Coach, known as the **Happiness In Love Coach** for coaching professional women to find true love and to bring balance to a happy relationship with a busy career.

Xiaoli moved from China to the US to work on her advanced degree. She reached for and quickly achieved success in her professional career, moving up through the ranks in corporate America. Yet, her personal life still suffered.

Having personally experienced two failed marriages and other broken relationships, Xiaoli set out on a quest to find happiness in life. She knew it was possible to achieve happiness in love while maintaining success in a professional career. But having both seemed quite elusive. After years of researching, learning, and coaching, Xiaoli cracked the "Happiness Code" and discovered what it takes for Asian professional women to find lasting happiness and love in the Western world while keeping their professional career on track. Captured in this book are those discoveries. It will teach you the necessary tools and skills to achieve balance in both your professional career and how to achieve a successful relationship.

Today, Xiaoli lives happily with her soulmate /Husband Jim and teach women from all cultural backgrounds on how to find their true love and what it takes to build a loving and lasting relationship.

THANK YOU!

Thank You for Reading My Book!

I really appreciate all of your feedback, and I love hearing what you have to say.

I need your input to make the next version of this book and my future books even better.

Please leave me a helpful review on Amazon letting me know what you thought of the book.

Thank you so much!
Xiaoli Mei

CONTACT INFORMATION

Email:	coachxiaoli@gmail.com
Phone:	925-457-2969
Website:	www.happinessinlove.com
Facebook:	www.facebook.com/Xiaoli.Mei
LinkedIn:	www.linkedin.com/in/xiaolimei
Instagram:	www.instagram.com/xiaoli.mei

Made in the USA
Middletown, DE
08 October 2022

12163188R00104